your REAL FOOD journey

Trina Holden

trinaholden.com

Contents

Forward

Five years ago when our family entered the "real food" movement, I went hog wild and pig crazy. I decided I was going to do it all. I read everything I could get my hands on and tried to implement it all immediately. Let me just tell you – I about drove myself off the deep end and I'm pretty sure my husband had repeated thoughts about sending me to the loony bin. My family would look at me weird. I got so bad I didn't even want to attend family events because I knew foods would be "sub-par" and not up to my REAL FOOD "HOLY" STANDARDS. (Insert my cocky nodding head right here.) I was alienating my family and driving myself nutso.

Can I tell you what happens to people after that sort of a start? BURNOUT – emotional and kitchen burn-out. After feeling like I was about to lose my mind, I realized it would make more sense to tackle one new change at a time – just one. Anyone can handle one, right? So, that became my method, one new food thing at a time.

I wish Trina's book had been around for me 5 years ago when I started...in fact, I found myself a little bit mad while reading it because it WASN'T there when I needed it. Her mantra, and the best way to come over to real food, is to only tackle one thing at a time. This is pure genius. Once you get one new thing under your belt and it's a habit, you'll be ready to tackle something else. Instead of trying it all at once and spending a good deal of time crying in your kitchen floor, rocking back and forth and holding a tub of coconut oil... like me.

This book is a breath of fresh air in the real food movement – not only is it simple and easy to follow, but it's so full of grace for every stage of your life. There is no guilt to be found here. There is only fantastic information, gentle guidance and encouragement. And lots of butter love. BUTTAH!

Let me just tell ya – I am not the poster child for real food. We eat out. Sometimes I buy my kids frozen waffles. I use canned tomatoes (GASP, the horror!). BUT I have found my sweet spot for real food. I have been making dairy kefir for five years. We avoid food coloring. I use butter like a boss and coconut oil is always melted and ready to go in my kitchen. We are happy where we are. Are you? If you can't honestly say YES! then you've come to the right place. Get ready for Trina to rock your kitchen and gently guide you toward better eating with a gentle dose of, "It's okay to eat at Chick-Fil-A sometimes."

You probably won't want to do everything in this book – and guess what? That's okay! Even Trina will tell you the same thing. If you were expected to agree with it all, that would make it the Bible. Ha! The point of the entire book, and what you'll quickly grasp, is that picking up a few simple changes will make a world of difference in your family's health and wellness. And what's not to love about someone who tells you to smother your broccoli in butter?

Congratulate yourself for reaching for this resource – you have made the first step. Or maybe you've already made the steps but find yourself in a food rut – congratulations, because you're also in the right spot! Trina speaks to us all...and guides us to steady progress. Let's do this together. Makes ya want to hold hands and sing Kumbayah, don't it?

~**Stacy Myers,** author of *Crock On!* and *Keep Crockin'*
stacymakescents.com

Introduction

Are you a real foodie? A crunchy mama? A whole food enthusiast?

Maybe you feel those titles don't apply to you. You think you have to have some level of expertise or years of success before earning the "Real Food Connoisseur" badge.

It's not like that!

I'm here to tell you there's no such thing as "arriving". Like so many other things, incorporating real food into your lifestyle is a journey, not a destination. And we're all in this together–those who eat all organic (I'm not there yet, I readily admit) to those who have just started reading labels to discern the real food from the fake. From the sourdough expert (again, not me!) to the gal who just made pancakes from scratch for the first time, we all have more to learn, and we all have something to share.

So, let's quit feeling like we're not crunchy enough to call ourselves "Real Foodies" and embrace the journey together.

A Step-by-Step Approach to Becoming a Real Foodie

At the beginning of this book, I want to share my most important tip for the process of incorporating real food into your lifestyle—the one tip I pass out to every friend who asks me for a recipe, or calls me overwhelmed at all they feel they need to learn and apply right away.

My top tip is based on the idea that making healthy changes for your family is a journey. You won't arrive all at once. It will be a process made up of days and weeks and small changes and gradually acquired new habits. You can embrace and enjoy the process of learning how to cook and eat real food, if you will take this long-term, slow and steady approach. So, here's the secret to steady progress:

Learn one new recipe, food source, or preparation technique at a time, and don't add another until that one becomes routine.

This means you shouldn't try to master yogurt and sourdough in the same week. Make yogurt on a regular basis until it becomes as brainless a task as throwing a load of laundry in your washer (which, hopefully, you've got down!). Only when you can practically do it in your sleep, should you move on to learning something new.

Here's another example: let's say this is the week you finally found a source for raw milk. Tuesday is pick-up day, and you don't remember until 4pm! You throw everybody in the car and race to the farm, hoping you haven't inconvenienced the dear farmer's wife with your tardiness. Next week, you plan it into the schedule (using a reminder app on your phone, maybe?) and you get there and get your milk with no sweat. The week after, something comes up and you completely forget to get milk at all. Whoops! But within a few more weeks, you've made it a habit.

Only then should you consider signing up for a weekly batch of vegetables from your local CSA.

If you don't take the step-by-step, "it's a journey" approach, you can very easily get overwhelmed and stressed and literally burn out and give up on real food altogether within a month. You have a much better chance at success if you make gradual progress with small changes that stick, rather than trying to do everything in one week!

This book is all about the slow, steady approach, teaching you ten real food basics and giving you a road map to find and reach your goals.

Finding Your Starting Point

People often ask me "How do I start getting more real food into my day?"

I usually answer with a question, "Well, where are you at?"

Your next step is largely defined by the progress you've already made. So let's look at the path behind us for a minute.

If this were a phone consultation, or we were chatting in real life, I'd ask you a series of questions to figure out just how much of what you're eating already qualifies as real food, and then share what, in my opinion, would be the next most important thing you should work on.

I might ask you, "What do you typically eat for breakfast?", or "How often do you eat grains?", or "Do you drink raw milk?", and we'd go from there. Because this is a book, I'm going to dive right in with some open-ended questions to get you thinking, and then go ahead and give you the ten most common suggestions I give people who want to make progress.

- Are you trying to eat healthier, but face constant cravings for sugar and caffeine?
- Do you struggle to lose weight no matter how much you focus on portion control and eating your vegetables?
- Do you have any signs that you are not digesting your food well (acid reflux, skin problems, constipation, food intolerances or allergies)?
- Do you already eat a nutritious diet, but wish you could make more from scratch so it doesn't cost you so much?

If you answered yes to any of those questions, then you're ready for these first ten steps on the real food journey.

Ten Key Steps on the Real Food Journey

Here are ten action steps I'd consider to be great places to start making changes in your diet and lifestyle. I've put them in a particular order for the sake of this book, and they are somewhat prioritized, but this is according to my opinion. You may deem #8 to be way more crucial than #3, and I'm totally okay with that! The purpose of this list is to help visualize the process, check off what you're already doing great on, and identify your next step toward wiser food choices for you and your family.

1. Get **fake foods** out your cupboards and off your shopping list.
2. Learn to **menu plan** and start building a list of real food meals you love.
3. Choose **good fats** and use them properly.
4. Make the **best dairy choices** for your family.
5. Learn how to **save money on meat** so you can afford higher quality.
6. Learn to make **bone broth** and enjoy it every day.
7. **Reduce grain consumption** and use wise preparation methods.
8. Switch to **natural sweeteners** and put sweets in their proper place.
9. Learn to **culture foods** and incorporate fermented superfoods into every meal.
10. Save time by learning the art of **bulk food preparation**.

Well, did you find your starting place? Remember, whether you're at #2 or #10 doesn't matter as much as your willingness to continue to make progress. (By the way, if you've conquered all ten, your next step is to call me and let me learn from you!)

Remember to look at these as steps to tackle one at a time, not a list to complete this week.

I hope that having this little "map", as it were, will help to "unwhelm" you a bit on your real food journey. But you know the really exciting part? I've got a chapter about each one of these steps so you aren't just stuck looking at a map, but you can actually start making some real progress!

Beginning the Journey

Spinach Salad with Berry Vinaigrette (pg. 92)

Real Food vs. Fake Food

All Natural. Gluten Free. No Sugar Added. No Preservatives.

Due to a growing interest in feeding ourselves better, the health food market has exploded in the last several years. The positive side of this is that real food and natural choices are becoming more and more readily available. The downside is that many companies are capitalizing on the trend and using clever marketing techniques to convince you that their product is the best thing you could put in your body.

But is it?

One of the first skills that you'll need on your real food journey is the ability to tell the real food from the fake impostors.

A Definition for Real Food

This starts, first of all, by defining what real food actually is. My personal definition, as I shared in the introduction to my first book, *Real {Fast} Food*, is:

> "...food as close to the way God created it as possible, free of additives and over-processing."

Many foods do have to be processed to some degree (peeled, ground, cooked, or fermented) in order to be eaten, but we should look for the most natural, traditional processes that change the food as little as possible from its original form.

The problem with a lot of what is marketed to us as "health food" is that it is so far from its original state that it's unrecognizable, both by our eyes and our bodies. We don't receive nutrition from fake food, so let's get it out of our diet! What I'd really like to do in this chapter is pull back the veil on some of the more popular "health" foods and encourage you to look and think twice before throwing things in your cart.

"Real Food" vs. "Fake Food"–which is it?

1. Milks made from grains and nuts

Nuts in their natural state are crunchy, hard, and brown. What did that poor nut have to go through to become a smooth, sweet, shelf-stable product? The answer: *a whole lot of processing*. A whole lot of additives for flavor and mouthfeel. Preservatives. Colorings. And the list goes on. The poor nut. This is what you call an identity crisis.

I know a lot of people choose milk alternatives because of dairy allergies, or because good milk isn't available, and believe they are making the best choice for their family. But I'd encourage you to first ascertain whether your dairy allergy is simply an inability to digest pasteurized and homogenized milk (which is missing the raw enzymes naturally found in milk that aid digestion), and second, ask yourself if highly processed milk substitutes really are the best thing to be drinking by the glassful.

Even the unsweetened versions of coconut or almond milk often contain synthetic vitamins which aren't recognized or metabolized by our bodies, and can actually put an unhealthy burden on our systems. Another common additive is carrageenan, which is toxic and inflammatory to our digestive system. I share these facts not to scare you, but to encourage you to see through marketing terms like "allergy friendly" and "all natural" and make informed decisions on what you feed your family in the name of health. Read labels. Look at all the added ingredients. Research the manufacturing process. You decide if this is real food. (We'll talk more about dairy options in Chapter 4.)

And to answer the question of whether milk substitutes are ever good for you–yes! If they are made at home with natural sweeteners and using techniques that aid digestion. The Healthy Home Economist* has several good recipes on her blog if you want make your own coconut, rice, or almond milk.

2. Vegetable oils

Again–I ask myself–who thought of making oil from beans? Do you know what that soybean went through to become a clear, oily fluid? Again–a whole lot of processing. Enough, in fact, that it changes the chemical makeup of the "food", meaning it loses the real food label, in my book. And did you know that "vegetable oil" is mainly made from soy (a "health food" fad from the 70s that should be avoided rather than embraced) or GMO corn? And that canola oil, made from rapeseed, is considered more toxic than soybeans?

You can get the lowdown on vegetable oils in the book, "*The Whole Soy Story*" by Kayla Daniels*. Suffice to say, they ought to be avoided at all cost. We'll talk about what to replace them with in Chapter 3.

3. Organic breakfast cereals

Do you know what extrusion is? It's the process most cold cereal products go through in order to make the batter into those perfect little shapes we love to slurp around on our spoon. But do you know what extrusion does? It uses such high temperatures and pressure that it practically makes the grains toxic. Also, have you looked at the ingredient list on most boxes of cold cereal? Some form of sweetener is almost always near the top. Even if it's natural, what you're doing is giving your body a highly processed, carb-rich bowlful—that at the least is going to give your blood sugar a rollercoaster ride for the rest of the morning, and at worst is going to burden your system with something it doesn't even recognize as food.

* For a list of all links and resources visit trinaholden.com/toolsforthejourney

Boxed cereals are an expensive, fake food that messes with our body's ability to function, rather than fueling us for the day. They should be avoided and replaced by genuine forms of fuel—like the breakfast ideas later in this book.

4. Gluten free and other allergy-friendly products

I hate to break it to you, but just because a food is labeled "gluten free" or is allergy friendly, doesn't mean it's automatically good for you. The fact is we're not just looking to feed ourselves stuff that won't give us an allergic reaction; we're looking for foods that will build our bodies, not just fill our stomachs. Often gluten free products are made with grain replacements like potato starch and tapioca that have an even crazier effect on our blood sugar than a wheat product. Foods with a high glycemic count (high in natural sugars) will not nourish us in the long term. Seeing an allergy-friendly label and automatically assuming it's good for you is overlooking the fact that our bodies need balanced forms of fuel in order to function well. Additionally, products that are dairy-free are often full of fake flavors and fillers to improve the taste. We're better off skipping that form of food (be it a bun or a scoop of ice "cream") and turning our focus to the real food that actually nourishes us.

We Must Read (and Understand!) the Labels

Education is the key to identifying real food versus fake food. We need to read and understand how food is labeled. We need to know all the different aliases for sugar and how MSG hides behind the phrase "natural flavoring". But it's not my place to give you a complete education in food labeling and how phrases like "all natural" have been abused. I simply want to gently remind you that all that glitters is not gold, and you must educate yourself on this journey. Google search "understanding ingredient lists" or "food label myths" so you know what to watch for. Wise choices go beyond choosing the organic label at the grocery store. As we attempt to feed our families well, let's make sure we start with real food–not over-processed, over-priced charlatans!

Stepping Stones
to Getting Rid of Fake Foods

* Look beyond the marketing on a product and read the ingredients list.
* Stop buying foods made with stuff you can't pronounce.
* Gradually replace favorite packaged foods with homemade variations.

Final Destination

The food we purchase is made with recognizable ingredients—things we could legitimately make in our own kitchen with whole foods.

1. pepperoni rolls
2. chicken divan
3. pizza
4. taco salad

A Minimalist Approach to Menu Planning

The second key step on our real food journey is learning the art of menu planning. Homemade, nutrient-dense meals are not just going to show up on the dinner table all by themselves. You have to think about your food in advance in order to have the ingredients you need when it's time to cook, and the time to build a meal from scratch. Having a menu plan is especially important in busy seasons when you can't afford to spend all day cooking or thinking about cooking.

But perhaps structure is not your strong suit. Maybe you operate best with a more free-spirited approach. Or maybe you kind of hate menu planning (like me). I have good news. Although I am capable of planning an entire month's worth of meals in one sitting (and I teach you how in my first cookbook, *Real {Fast} Food*), I have since found a faster, more flexible approach to meal planning that I use when life circumstances–or even just my mood–aren't conducive to a rigid schedule.

Flexible Menu Planning in Less Than Ten Minutes

The first is to jot down at least three dinners that sound appetizing in the next week. I do this on a scrap of envelope or cardboard if I can't find a notebook. If this feels like menu planning, trick yourself and call it a "wish list". I try to choose meals that are appropriate to the season, but sometimes I just don't feel like it. So there.

Get meal ideas from:
- recipes you've pinned on Pinterest
- a magazine
- a new cookbook
- your favorite eCookbook
- call a friend and hijack her menu plan (I've totally done this)
- poll Facebook (always eye-opening!)

Next, add a few more family favorites to your wish list. You know, those meals you find yourself making every week because no one complains about seeing them again and again? (Our weekly favorites are home-made pizza, anything wrapped in a tortilla, and all things grilled.)

Now, jot down three breakfast ideas. That's all you'll need because you're going to have each of them twice, and on the seventh day, we're going to be spontaneous.

Optionally: if your lunches need to be packable, jot down three lunch ideas. But if you usually eat lunch at home–you get to skip this step! Lunches will be leftovers.

Okay, that's it. *You just made a week's meal plan*. In less than ten minutes. *And you still have brains cells left.*

What's that? That doesn't look like much of a plan? Don't worry, it's enough–the rest is in the execution…

How to Execute Your Flexible Meal Plan

Once a week:

- Quickly think through each meal on your "wish list" and jot down the ingredients you need to buy in order to create that meal. If you have a robust pantry and freezer, you may only need an item or two to complete each meal. If you haven't shopped in a while, well then, *it's a good thing you're making this list, right*?

- Go shopping and buy the stuff you need for the meals you're in the mood for. Add or replace items in your cart if you see a good sale. The key is to be let your list guide, but not bind you!

- Bring food home (elementary, I know). If you bought fresh meat, check the expiration date and toss it in the freezer if you don't think you'll be in the mood for it before it expires.

Daily:

Okay, now comes the most important part of being a free-spirited meal planner: for just six minutes each day, *you will have to think ahead*. Just six minutes and then we can go back to being spontaneous as larks, alright? And these six minutes are divided in two different segments, *so I know we can do it*.

- **First three minutes**: As you're making breakfast each morning, look at your day and make an educated guess how much time you'll have to prep dinner, and what meal from your wish list fits the day's mood and food requirements. Once you've decided, do one small thing to help prepare for that meal, like pulling meat out of the freezer, making salad dressing, or starting some dough to soak or rise. I've found that if I think about dinner just a little bit in advance and do just a teensy bit of advance preparation, the task of getting it on the table is much more natural and less stressful. It sometimes even feels fun. *You've been warned.*

- **Second three minutes**: As you're cleaning up dinner, decide what you feel like for breakfast the next morning. Again, do one small thing to facilitate that meal before you leave the kitchen–setting pantry ingredients out, soaking grains, or even just pulling out a recipe. When you wake the next morning, the hardest part of breakfast (trying to decide what to make while you're still asleep) will be past you. It's a feeling nearly as good as that first sip of coffee (or so I imagine, as a non-coffee drinker).

If you'll take ten minutes a week to quickly brainstorm a few meal ideas, shop with a list, and incorporate just six minutes of forethought into each day, you will be setting yourself up for success in feeding your family well, and you don't have to change your personality to do it.

Do you think this flexible plan would work for you? Here's what some of my readers had to say about a flexible meal plan...

"I've been doing something similar for a while now, and love how much it helps – without making me feel 'fenced in' to certain meals on certain days. I thrive on spontaneity in the kitchen, but picking out a few meals for the week, rather than plunking them on specific days, helps save time and money. I can plan around whatever excess we have in the pantry, and then match coupons up for those meal ideas. It also reminds me to ask hubby for any requests he has, and run new recipe ideas by him (since he's kind of a picky eater)."
—Elizabeth

"I've tried all manner of menu plans. Right now I plan for the month, but shop for the week. Knowing that Friday is pizza night, Saturday is chocolate chip pancake night (thanks to hubby!), and Sunday is your pick night, only leaves me with four meals a week to plan. My kids love the routine of Friday-Sunday meals and I love that the meals take little effort on my part."
—Stephanie

"I should probably give this a try – everything works so much better when I plan things! We're currently on week three of a three-week plan which has been working pretty well, mostly because we don't feel obliged to stick to it and we shift things from day to day as needed."
—Cathrijn

Stepping Stones

to Having a Menu Plan That Works for You

- Jot down a list of favorite recipes—have your family contribute their picks!
- Make your grocery list with future meals in mind, not just a list of what you've run out of.
- Start by planning one meal, one day in advance. Grow from there.
- Practice adding three minutes of future meal prep to your evening and morning routines.

Final Destination

The habit of thinking about your meals in advance, and the ability to plan a week at a time if necessary.

Frugal, Flavorful Chili (pg. 82)

Embracing Good Fats

Sometimes the real food journey becomes an adventure–what you're learning excites you, the new foods you try are delicious, and your body's response is immediate.

That's what I experienced when I discovered the truth about good fats versus bad fats.

When I began to embrace the idea that our body actually needs fat to function well, and added good fats like full fat dairy products, coconut oil, and plenty of butter into my daily menu, I felt the results immediately! Cravings subsided as my body finally received the fuel it was craving. Losing my baby weight never became an issue. And, when I learned which fats were good for cooking, and which ones shouldn't be overheated, I quit having gallbladder attacks! All this from adding something easy and tasty to my meals!

There's a lot of confusion about fats, though–even among people who are making a genuine effort to make healthy food choices. Here are three myths you should be aware of, and how to make good fats a great part of your menu.

Myth #1: Fat is Bad

Truth: Fat is essential to our bodies functioning well! Your brain is two-thirds fat, your hormone system runs on fat, and your cells are comprised of 50% fat. Good fats provide energy, help satiate your appetite, and are a carrier for fat-soluble vitamins A, D, E, and K. We cannot function well without good fats in our diet.

Myth #2: Vegetable Oil is a Healthy Fat

Truth: Turning a vegetable (often GMO corn or the toxic soybean) into an oil is a highly-involved process of bleaching, deodorizing, and treating with chemicals. The resulting oils are high in polyunsaturated fatty acids, which are linked to free radical damage and degenerative conditions like autoimmune disorders and Alzheimer's.

Sorry, I got a little geeky on you there, but you need to know the truth: vegetable oils are not food, and are never good for you.

Myth #3: We Should Limit Fat in our Diets

Truth: Actually, most of us aren't getting enough fats! We need fats to assimilate certain vitamins, nourish our hormone system, and regulate blood sugar, among other things. If you aren't getting enough of good fats, your body will actually feel like it's starving, and will kick into "survival mode"—storing whatever food you do eat as body fat as if in preparation for a famine. If you are not giving your body the fuel it needs in the way of good fats, you can be literally starving your system even as you gain weight!

So, are you ready for this step–embracing good fats in your diet, and using them properly?

Choosing and Using the Right Fats

Just like in every area of real food, our guide to choosing the proper fats is seeking out oils and fats that are as close to the way God made them as possible. The oils themselves clue us in to their proper uses. Naturally saturated fat from plants grown in warmer climates or made from animal products that are solid at cooler temperatures and melt when exposed to heat are best for cooking. These include:

- Butter—baking, eating
- Lard (from pigs)—baking, deep-frying
- Tallow (from beef)—cooking, deep-frying, sautéing
- Coconut oil—baking, deep-frying, sautéing, mayonnaise, smoothies, eating
- Palm shortening—baking, frying

Oils from plants grown in cooler climates that are naturally liquid should not be heated (as they so often are as part of the industry's refining processes). These oils should be used for salad dressings and as a dietary supplement to ensure we get enough Omega 3 fatty acids. Look for extra virgin, cold-pressed (not expeller pressed or partially hydrogenated).

- Olive oil—salad dressings, mayonnaise
- Flaxseed oil—in smoothies, dressings, or taken by the spoonful
- Cod liver oil—in capsules, or by the spoonful
- Sunflower oil—dressings, mayonnaise
- Sesame oil—dressings, mayonnaise

What Do Good Fats Look Like in My Kitchen?

We often consume a pound of butter a day, from frying our eggs in the morning, to buttering our bread at lunch, and to making a creamy white sauce with dinner. We aren't afraid of fat in this kitchen, oh no! I use coconut oil often in baking (gently melting it and using it wherever vegetable oil is called for) and I dollop a spoonful into smoothies to help the natural sugars in the fruit hit our blood sugar more gradually. I buy the cheaper, more refined coconut oil for deep-frying. I reserve olive oil for salad dressings and mayonnaise, and occasionally supplement it with sesame and sunflower oils for flavor variations.

One of the challenges I've faced in my journey to using healthy fats in nourishing ways is what to do with meat marinades that require a liquid fat to mix in with the other ingredients, but then sit in the fridge where the fat solidifies. I had made the switch from vegetable to olive oil for all my marinades, but then realized that the environment of a grill was too hot for olive oil! So I have experimented with mixing all the marinade ingredients except the oil, and adding gently warmed coconut oil to the mix right before it's time to put the meat on the grill. This seems to work great so far, and our favorite marinades are just as yummy. You can use the more refined coconut oil wherever the flavor of coconut oil wouldn't be quite right.

Perhaps the most challenging aspect of embracing good fats is that they are either very expensive or unavailable locally. This is most often the case with coconut oil, which I order in bulk online to get a reasonable price for a level of quality which I can't get locally. I buy my coconut oil by the gallon a few times a year, and source my other fats from local stores, watching for sales on butter and olive oil. I make my own butter occasionally when I have access to lots of good cream, but otherwise rest in using store-bought butter. Raw butter made from cows that are eating fresh grass would be ideal, but at this point in our real food journey, store-bought butter is the best I can do. It's still better than margarine!

Good Fats Were God's Idea

"Then he said unto them, Go your way, *eat the fat*, and drink the sweet, and send portions unto them for whom nothing is prepared: for this day is holy unto our Lord: neither be ye sorry; for the joy of the LORD is your strength." Nehemiah 8:10 (emphasis mine)

God encourages us to embrace good fats! He created our bodies, and knows what is good for us. Proverbs 13:4, 11:25, and 21:20 also put fat in a positive light. Learning how fat actually helps our bodies assimilate certain nutrients and supports a myriad of body functions right down to the cellular level, has caused me to marvel at how God provided for this need with a variety of fats present in nature. It's sad when we avoid fats and strip things like milk of all their fat content, thinking we can improve on God's design. Let's trust His design and eat the fat!

Small Changes—Big, Fat Difference

Here's a conversation I had with a friend when I originally posted this information on my blog. Our discussion demonstrates just how small and simple making changes in this area can be, and yet what a significant effect it can have on our bodies:

Mandy: "I struggle with gallbladder issues *all* the time and have refused to have it removed. Are you saying that using olive oil to fry veggies with is *not* a good thing? So a simple step I can take right now is to use olive oil when it's *not* being heated and butter for when I do heat something up?"

Trina: "Yes, Mandy! I quit having gallbladder attacks when I quit frying in olive oil. I know frying in and grilling with olive oil is common practice, but light sautéing or short baking times is all that olive oil can handle without becoming difficult to digest. Fats go straight to the liver to be dealt with, and if we're not preparing the right fats in the right way, it can overburden our poor gallbladder. There is relief, and it may be as simple as switching what you fry in! I love frying in butter, or a more refined coconut oil that doesn't have a strong coconut taste–that's my go-to these days for frying. It's so yummy, and much cheaper than a quality olive oil!"

Are you ready to make some fat changes? For more resources to help you wrap your mind around this step visit trinaholden.com/toolsforthejourney

to Embracing Good Fats

- Use up or get rid of any over-processed, unhealthy oils in your pantry or refrigerator.
- Find a source for cold-pressed, extra virgin coconut oil.
- See if you can find or afford local butter from grass fed cows.
- Try making your own butter if you have access to raw cream.
- Learn to put a generous pat of butter on your steamed vegetables, hot breakfast cereal, and anywhere else you crave it.
- Choose full fat dairy products and avoid the "low fat" label on any product you buy!
- Try making your own mayonnaise and salad dressings (recipes in Part Two).

Final Destination

All of the fats you consume are in their most natural, least refined state, and low-temp oils are not used for cooking.

Easiest Yogurt Recipe Ever (pg. 20)

The Best Dairy for Your Family

I think I could write a whole book about our family's adventures with milk! I'm just going to give you the highlights here (and a few low spots) because it gives a great glimpse into how the process of making healthier choices for your family really is a journey—with progress, pit stops, detours, and discoveries.

I grew up drinking soy and rice milk. I am truly grateful for the effort my mom put into learning about health food and feeding us as best she knew how, but modern studies have shown us what a poor and even dangerous substitute soy products are, *and* just how essential good, raw milk is to a nourishing diet.

I had my first taste of real, raw cow's milk in my teens, when my family moved to a working homestead where it was cheap and in abundance. We cooked with it and made yogurt, but I didn't start drinking it by the glassful until after I was married and studying nutrition for my own family. This stuff was good and good for you! Although raw milk wasn't technically legal for sale where we were living at the time, we were in the middle of rural farm country and I found a neighboring farmer more than willing to share fresh milk straight from his bulk tank. This made "better dairy choices" one of the easiest steps on my real food journey!

I became passionate about raw milk. Besides drinking a glass with nearly every meal, I experimented with yogurt, kefir, and even soft cheeses. The more I learned about raw milk, the more we drank, until my little family was using four gallons a week! I even tried the "Milk Cure"—drinking nothing but raw milk for six days as a gentle cleanse and rest for my digestive tract. It felt like we had this aspect of a nourishing diet down pat.

Then our business took us to Alabama temporarily and raw milk was nowhere to be found! Suddenly our journey to good dairy for our family took a significant backtrack—the only milk we could find was ultra-pasteurized and homogenized from the local supermarket. I opted for the organic brand and limited our use to just cooking and yogurt making. Whenever we traveled home we binged on good milk again, and each time we traveled south we brought as many gallons as possible back in a giant cooler, savoring it till it was gone.

Eventually we found a local dairy that sold un-homogenized, low-temp pasteurized milk from grass fed cows. This was a significant improvement over what the supermarket was offering, so we built a stop at the dairy into our weekly routine, and though we still missed drinking raw milk by the glassful, I was grateful that at least we were avoiding the evils of homogenization.

Then came the day we officially made Alabama our new home. There was no more possibility for imported milk from the North, and the longer we went without it, the more we missed it. My husband and I especially noticed more cravings for junk food and sweets when our bodies weren't receiving the deep nutrition that four gallons of fresh milk from grass fed cows had been providing our diets each week.

This desperation led us to do something I never thought I'd do—cross the border to shop for milk! We found a farm selling raw milk as pet food in Georgia and made the two and a half hour round trip as a treat for my birthday. Once we tasted the raw milk again, and discussed how important we felt it was for our family, my husband and I agreed that we would make this a monthly thing and bring back ten gallons at a time to freeze and thaw as needed.

We're back up to consuming about four gallons a week again—two from the local dairy which I use for yogurt, kefir, and in cooking, and two gallons of the delicious raw milk for drinking.

So, that's our dairy journey. We've had ups and downs, and we've certainly not arrived yet. I still buy most of our other dairy products at the supermarket because our budget can't handle the cost of raw cheese, and my schedule can't handle churning our own butter right now. Those are goals to shoot for, but meanwhile I'm grateful that with a little creativity and effort we've been able to make continued progress.

Why All the Trouble for Raw Milk?

By this time you're probably thinking "this lady is crazy!" and "why all this trouble for raw milk?!" Well, there's a host of reasons, not the least of which are:

Pasteurization is damaging to milk and unnecessary under proper conditions. Pasteurization was implemented in the early 1900's to curtail the spread of diseases like tuberculosis which were caused by contaminated milk. But today's higher levels of sanitation, improved refrigeration, routine testing, and the ability to know your farmer can set your mind at ease about raw milk. Pasteurization kills the naturally occurring enzymes in milk, making it harder to digest and leaving fewer nutrients available for assimilation.

Homogenization is reportedly even worse—the molecular structure of the milk is actually changed under the high pressure of the homogenization process. How detrimental this is has been hotly debated (some argue it's the cause of heart disease, others blame it for ulcers), but I believe we should be cautious of any food that has undergone such high amounts of processing.

Raw milk, on the other hand, is the ultimate healthy convenience food. Once you gone through the effort to source and to pick it up, you now have a super-food in your fridge that requires no additional effort or preparation to enjoy. You just pour yourself a glassful! The balance of fats, proteins and carbohydrates give it a low glycemic index and make it the perfect satiating snack. Plus, if it's from cows on pasture, you're getting a huge dose in nutrients from all that good green grass and sunshine the cows enjoy. When my little ones are drinking milk from grass fed cows, I don't freak out as much about their disinterest in salads and vegetables. The Lord has provided multiple ways for us to receive good nutrition, and raw milk is an incredible gift.

Another benefit to raw milk is that it allows you to make high-quality dairy products for your family. I regularly make all our family's yogurt and kefir at a fraction of the cost of a comparable product in the store. Things like butter and sour cream cost a bit more in expense and effort, so I don't make them as often, but when I do, the finished product is far superior to anything I can find on store shelves.

How to Find Raw Milk in Your Area:

The best way to find raw milk is by word of mouth. Start with other people you know who are into healthy eating. If they've found raw milk, they'll probably be more than willing to introduce you to their farmer. (That's how I found my original source up North.) However, if they don't have a source, you'll have to look further.

Stop at your local farmers market, bulk food store, produce stand or—if you're lucky—your Amish neighbor. These folks are usually more connected to their food supply and they have a community mindset, making them a great source for this kind of information.

Your next option is the RealMilk.com website. Their database is by no means exhaustive, but they list availability and regulations for raw milk in each state, and list contact information for many reputable farms. When we moved to Alabama, I spent hours online with RealMilk.com and Google Maps open, checking for the farms nearest to me, and calling for availability and pricing. This is how we found our supply in Georgia.

If that doesn't turn up any leads, you could simply head into the country and stop at the first farm you see that has cows in the pasture. Go around milking time (5-7, AM or PM) to be sure to catch someone around the barn. Introduce yourself and tell them you love to drink raw milk and support local farmers and are looking for a source for a few gallons a week. All they can say is "no", then you hop in the car and drive on. Don't forget to ask them if they know of someone who might say yes!

The search for raw milk is made challenging in many states due to regulations against the sale of raw milk. Sometimes you can work around these laws with cow shares, selling the milk labeled as pet food, or bartering. You will have to decide how far you will go to put raw milk in your diet. No matter where you live, you do have the option of buying frozen raw milk and having it shipped to you, but this is certainly the most costly way to purchase milk, leaving us with the question:

What Do I Do If I Can't Find or Afford Raw Milk?

Option #1: Store-bought, pasteurized, homogenized milk from conventional farms.

Because the extreme process and high heat of homogenization literally changes the chemical makeup of the milk, this is the least preferable option in my book. Plus, even what's labeled "whole milk" in stores does not have the full butterfat content of whole milk in its natural state. When what was on the shelves at the store was the only option for us, I bought a half gallon of organic milk at a time, and only used it for cooking or culturing. We didn't drink it by the glassful.

If store-bought milk is your only option, I recommend buying the best label you can afford with the highest fat content available and culturing it–making it into kefir or yogurt–to make it easier to digest. In order to get the amount of calcium, saturated fats, and other good stuff our bodies need from dairy, get intentional about sourcing and enjoying the best sour cream, cheese, yogurt, butter, and other milk products you can afford. (Good quality dairy products like raw cheese and grass fed butter are usually more readily available than raw milk.)

Option #2: Non-homogenized, low-temp pasteurized milk.

This is what my family consumed for nearly two years in Alabama before we chose to drive to Georgia for milk. Now, this is still not ideal because it's missing the enzymes that help you digest the fats and sugars in the milk, but it *is* a better option than homogenization. Just as when we were buying store-bought milk, I limited our consumption of it by the glassful because we found we didn't digest it as well and it triggered some congestion. But I bought two gallons a week and made all our yogurt and kefir with it for the summers we were in Alabama. I served kefir smoothies every morning, and we had yogurt with at least one meal a day to make up for the fact that we weren't drinking milk by the glassful like we did back in New York.

This milk was $5 a gallon, which may seem steep to you. However, because I was using it to make our yogurt, it was actually saving us money–one quart of whole fat yogurt was $3+ at the store, but I could make it for $1.25/qt.

If low-temp pasteurized milk is what's available to you, embrace it and, once again, make sure to culture as much of it as possible.

Option #3: Get a Goat.

Sounds extreme, but you have no idea how serious I am. Raw milk is such a huge part of the diet my family thrives on, it's important enough to me that I have plans to get my own milk-producing animal if it becomes necessary. A goat (or two) would be my choice because they are smaller and cheaper than cows and my children would be able to help with the care and chores.

I know this is not an option for many people, but it is worth considering if you have a little bit of land and some children to help with chores or friends willing to co-op on the responsibilities.

Doing the Best with What You Have

With raw milk–and any other aspect of the real food journey–it all comes down to doing the best you can with what you have, and not stressing about what you can't control. One of the most beneficial ways you can enjoy milk is by culturing it. No matter what milk you have in your fridge, you can make progress on your journey today by learning to make yogurt!

Easiest Yogurt Recipe {Ever!}

I have been making yogurt off and on for nearly twenty years. I have had my share of failed batches, gloppy results, and troubleshooting. Over the years I've refined the recipe to be as simple as possible so it still fits into my ever-more-complicated life as a wife and mom to a growing family.

Warning: You will need no fancy equipment to make this yogurt. None at all. Just a pot, a quart jar with a lid, and a thermometer—but even the thermometer is optional. How cool is that?

This recipe involves heating the milk, and uses a small amount of plain, store-bought yogurt as a starter. It is possible to make raw yogurt, but it requires a different starter that usually has to be mail-ordered. So, we're going to stick with the simplest method you can make with stuff you probably already have on hand.

Step 1: Heating

Pour milk into a large saucepan. The amount you use is up to you–I usually make three quarts of yogurt at a time, because that's about how much yogurt we will eat before it would spoil (your homemade yogurt will last two to three weeks.) Heat milk to 185°F, or until it's simmering–small bubbles will come to the surface, and it will begin to form a "skin" on top. This is called scalding the milk. Once it reaches this point, remove the milk from the heat.

Step 2: Sterilizing

Pour the hot milk straight into the jars you want your finished yogurt in. I use gallon or quart jars. Use whatever size you want, but do use glass. I used to sterilize the jars separately, but realized that pouring the scalding hot milk into the jars effectively sterilizes them and saves me–and you!–a whole step. Sterilizing is important to make sure you control which bacteria grows during incubation. Starting with sterilized jars and milk means that only the good bacteria you add with the starter is alive and growing.

Step 3: Cooling

Before you add your starter, you need to let the milk cool until you can comfortably dip your finger into it–warm, but not burning you. (This is about 115°F if you must know, but I like skipping the thermometer and just using my finger–saves me another thing to wash.)

If you don't want to wait the hour or two for the milk to cool, you can hurry up this step by putting your jars into a saucepan or dishpan of cold tap water. I like to do this because this shrinks my yogurt-making session to about the length of time it takes me to make and serve a meal, and I'm less likely to leave the kitchen and forget about it. Just keep checking the milk, because it cools pretty fast in the cool water bath.

Step 4: Adding starter

When milk has cooled to a tolerable temperature, it's time to add your starter. This is simply a bit of plain, store-bought yogurt, or yogurt saved from your last batch. You will need 2-3 T. per quart jar, or ½ c. for a gallon. Stir the yogurt gently into the milk in the jars–emphasis on gently as you're introducing the yogurt to the milk, not incorporating.

Step 5: Incubation

In this step we are providing a warm, nurturing environment for your starter to flourish and effectively culture your milk. Cap jar(s), and set into your saucepan or dish pan again. This time, fill the pan up with the hottest water you can get from your tap. You want the hot water to reach up to the level of the milk in the jars. This is how you will incubate your yogurt. Leave on counter 8-12 hours (all day, if you make it in the morning, all night if you make this before bed). At the end of that time, transfer the yogurt to your fridge to cool.

This is by far the easiest method of incubating yogurt, but it works best if you have really hot tap water and are making at least two quarts of yogurt at a time. Smaller batches won't retain the amount of heat long enough for the cultures to flourish. For smaller batches of yogurt, you may want to experiment with incubating the milk in a cooler filled with hot water, or wrapping the jars in a heating pad on the counter for the same amount of time.

The finished yogurt will have thickened and have some separated whey on top. It will firm up further in the fridge.

The resulting yogurt is so thick and creamy, you'll be amazed. And, you'll notice I don't add anything to my yogurt–no sweeteners or flavor. That's because around here, yogurt is usually a vehicle for fresh or frozen fruit or other yummy additives, and we find we don't need the sweetener. If you do want to make a sweeter, vanilla-flavored yogurt, you'll find a simple method for vanilla yogurt in *Real {Fast} Food*.

How to Make Kefir {The Simplest Cultured Dairy}

If you want the benefits of cultured dairy, but yogurt is a bit too involved for you or the season of life you're in—good news! Kefir is the easiest cultured dairy—it literally only takes five minutes every three days to always have kefir in your kitchen!

Kefir is a slightly runnier cousin to yogurt. It is very similar to yogurt in that it has lots of probiotics and good bacteria, but with the added benefit of friendly yeast cultures. If you have trouble digesting other forms of dairy, kefir may be your new best friend! Like yogurt, kefir can be made with whatever milk you have available to you—as long as it's from an animal. (Vegan kefir made with coconut or almond milk requires a different starter.) Kefir can be used in baking, soaking grains, smoothies, and even just plain, drunk from a glass. The main difference between kefir and yogurt is that kefir starter, called grains, can't be bought in your local dairy aisle. But don't worry, it's not that hard to find some…

Where to get kefir grains

- Option #1 Get them from a friend. Kefir grains multiply every time you make a batch and can be divided and shared, so if you've got a friend who makes kefir, you already have a source!
- Option #2 If you don't have a friend or a friend of a friend to get some grains from, I suggest looking on Craigslist, or asking around at your local farmers market, co-op, health food store, or any place crunchy people congregate.
- Option #3 If that fails, you can order grains online from a source like CulturesforHealth.com.

A final strategy, if you're impatient to try this fantastic cultured dairy, is to purchase powdered kefir starter–this is more readily available and can often be found at your grocery or health food store. The powdered starter can't be used repeatedly like the grains–you have to keep buying the packets. But otherwise it tastes the same and is equally nutritious. (You can find the instructions for making kefir with powdered starter on my blog.)

Step 1: Culturing

Pour milk into a quart jar with your kefir grains. Screw on a lid (some people use a coffee filter with a rubber band—I haven't found this necessary) and leave on counter at room temperature until it firms up. How fast your kefir cultures will depend on the grains and the temperature in your house—it can take anywhere from 12 hours to three days. When you tip the jar over and see that the milk has clumped into a firm glob, it's done.

Step 2: Straining

You will want to strain your grains out of the finished kefir before eating the kefir, or you'll not have anything to start the next batch with! Kefir doesn't like metal utensils or sieves, so find a plastic colander to strain them through, and use a plastic spatula when working with your kefir. I strain my grains through a plastic sieve, letting the finished kefir drip into a bowl. The grains will appear like gelatinous clumps of cauliflower—slightly less opaque than clumps of kefir.—set these aside. Pour the strained kefir back into the jar it incubated in and store it in the fridge. The kefir grains go into a fresh, clean jar with more milk and go onto a shelf in my pantry to make another batch.

It's that simple!

Caring for your kefir grains

Kefir grains look like cauliflower and are similar in texture to tapioca pearls–slightly firm and gummy. Each time you use the grains, they will reproduce, allowing you to eventually split your grains and share them with others. You need about two tablespoons of grains to culture a quart of milk.

For the first year I had my grains, they were reproducing soooo slowly, I rarely had enough to divide and share them. Then a friend pointed out that the holes in my colander might be too big and the little baby grains were probably all going through the holes! I switched colanders and, sure enough, my grains began to multiply.

Because the finished kefir is sometimes nearly as thick as yogurt, I usually have to help the straining process along by banging the colander against the sides of my bowl. (Bang! Bang! Bang! "What's that sound?" "Oh, just Mommy making kefir!")

If at any time you don't want to make another batch of kefir immediately, you can put your grains on hold in a small glass jar with just enough milk to cover them. They keep in the fridge for months this way. This is also what I do with my kefir when traveling. To begin using them again, just pour the grains and the milk (which will have grown thick) into a larger jar, add milk, and put it on the counter to begin culturing again!

How We Enjoy Kefir

We consume over a gallon of cultured dairy each week, and I make more kefir than yogurt because it's faster and easier to make. The primary use is in our breakfast smoothies–I like the flavor and consistency of kefir smoothies even better than yogurt. The other main thing I use it in is soaking my baked goods. My tortilla dough, pizza dough, bread dough, pancake batter, and favorite muffin recipes all call for some form of cultured dairy, and I primarily use kefir because it's a little runnier and pours into a recipe easier.

Some people drink kefir plain–I'm not a fan, it's just a little too tart for me to drink by itself. But we still manage to consume several cups a day. This morning's blender pancakes included kefir, and kefir will also be a key component to the peanut butter chocolate smoothie I'm craving for this afternoon's snack.

I think it's safe to say my kitchen literally runs on kefir.

How to Make Whey

The final dairy product we'll discuss in this chapter is whey. Whey is the clear, yellowish liquid that separates from milk when it is cultured. Whey has many uses in the real food kitchen, including soaking grains, making lacto-fermented drinks and condiments, and starting batches of sauerkraut and other fermented veggies. In other words, you're going to use this on your real food journey!

Thankfully, whey kind of makes itself while you're making other things, so it's not a hard to come by. There are two places to find whey in your kitchen:

Whey from yogurt:

That clear, yellowish liquid that collects on the top of yogurt while it sits in the fridge? That's whey! You can harvest it by scooping yogurt into a cheesecloth-lined colander and letting it sit for a few hours. A small amount of whey will drip from the yogurt and will be just enough to for your next batch of mayonnaise or sauerkraut. You can strain kefir to get whey, as well.

Whey from raw milk:

If you have access to raw milk, you can "clabber" it to harvest larger amounts of whey. This means you simply leave a jar of raw milk on the counter at room temperature until it separates. Clabbering will take one to four days depending on the room's temperature. When the milk gets all chunky and is floating around in clear, yellowish liquid, it's clabbered and you can strain it through cheesecloth. A quart of milk will produce about two to three cups whey, and one to two cups of thick raw cream cheese. Yes, you just made cream cheese! Store both in the fridge—the cream cheese will last a week or two, and the whey is good for up to six months. (You can tell when cultured dairy products have gone bad—they will smell bad instead of just sour.)

Hopefully by now you've seen just how important and yet simple the switch to better dairy products can be. It's a significant step on the real food journey to transition to traditional forms of dairy and learn how to culture them yourself. The recipes in this section only scratch the surface of what you can do with a gallon of raw milk—sour cream, butter, buttermilk, and soft cheeses are easily made at home! Harder cheeses require specific cultures and a bit more equipment, but may be a goal you want to pursue. Just remember to start small and move on only after your new skills have become routine.

Stepping Stones

to Better Dairy Choices

- Switch to buying full fat dairy products, and unhomogenized if you can find it.
- Learn the raw milk regulations for your state and find a local source if available.
- Sample raw milk if you never have before!
- Do the math and calculate how much it will save your family each month if you made your own yogurt.
- See if you can track down some kefir grains in your area.
- Strain some yogurt for whey so you can make the lacto-fermented mayonnaise.

Final Destination

All milk and dairy products sourced from grass fed animals, consumed raw and/or cultured.

How to Afford Better Quality Meat for Your Family

The idea of buying organic, grass fed beef or chicken can be intimidating. Isn't that stuff really *expensive*? Well, yes, but even our family, during our tightest budgeted seasons, have been able to afford grass fed beef or better quality poultry with these four tips:

1. Choose the cheapest cuts.

Bone-in is cheaper than boneless. (And you can make nutritious broth with those bones!) Ground beef beats steak every time. Short ribs are delicious braised, and are usually the cheapest item the butcher offers. Steak is not a "must" for special occasions. There are plenty of special occasion entrees made with ground beef:

- Meatloaf (I wrap ours in bacon for company!)
- Salisbury steaks with gravy from pan drippings
- Chili with all the fixings
- Cheeseburger soup
- Burgers
- Enchiladas
- Taco bar

Chicken is always cheaper when you buy it whole and cut it up yourself. I regularly buy two to three roasters at a time. In the winter, I will bake them whole, serving roast chicken one night, and then eat the leftover, deboned chicken in soups and casseroles for days. In the summer, I cut up the chicken, putting our favorite dark meat portions into marinades for the grill, and chopping the breast meat into bite-sized pieces for quick, summertime stir-fries or homemade chicken tenders. Summer or winter, the wings always get cut off and tossed into a bag in the freezer till we have enough for wing night! This method means I get all our chicken at the cheapest price per pound, while still ensuring lots of variety in our menu.

2. Buy the meat unseasoned and unformed.

Pre-made meatballs (if you can find them without junky additives and fillers) are going to be more expensive than buying ground beef and forming your own meatballs. Pre-formed burgers are more expensive, again, than just the ground beef. You save by shaping and seasoning the meat yourself.

Shaped or sliced meats like turkey breast, hams, and roast beef can be found without additives, but the price per pound skyrockets. Learn to put leftover barbequed meat or meatloaf on sandwiches or wraps to avoid this most expensive form of meat.

3. Buy in bulk.

Always choose the club pack over the smaller package. I know that much meat can be intimidating, but you *will* eat it all eventually. Go for the club pack if you're at the supermarket, and divide it up into meal-sized portions yourself when you get home, freezing what you won't eat this week. You'll also save yourself additional trips to the store because you can grab meat for dinner out of the freezer.

Pasture-raised chickens can be crazy expensive, but if you find a small business or family farm, they often have discounts if you buy ten birds or more, or are willing to buy frozen birds from last season. I was raised on a natural chicken farm and we loved the customers who bought ten to twenty birds at a time—bulk purchases save work for the farmer, and that's why they're often willing to pass on some savings to you.

We recently were able to buy half a cow for the first time, for $4.50/lb. That means the ground beef was $4.50/lb…but then, so were all of the lovely, grass fed roasts and steaks! Hooray! I'm really excited to have some variety in our freezer for a change, and we could afford steaks because we bought a whole chunk of the cow at once.

4. Go straight to the source.

One of the best ways to save on meat is to eliminate the middle man. Go straight to the source–your nearest butcher or farmer—and order a portion of meat straight from him. (Yes, local butchers still exist, but you won't find them next to Target. You're going to have to make a few phone calls or do a little internet research.) Often the price of meat straight from the butcher is not much more than what you're paying for the higher quality options at the store. If even a quarter of a cow (30 to 50 pounds) is too much meat for you to buy or store at once, find a few friends to split it with you.

Another advantage of going to the source is you may find that though you thought you were just making the trip for, say, some organic chickens, you find they have eggs, local honey, or produce from their garden, too. Suddenly you've jumped ahead three spaces on the journey to finding and buying locally grown food!

For me, the biggest challenge to feeding my family better meat has been sourcing it, and then changing my buying habits. But usually the sourcing is a one-time effort comprised of a little detective work, all with a smartphone from the comfort of my couch. Learning to make an extra stop each month at the butcher (or saving up to buy a half a cow) instead of getting all my groceries at the one-stop-shop supermarket is an adjustment that soon becomes routine. And then, suddenly, I've formed a real food habit and taken another successful step in my real food journey.

My Readers Chime In

"If you've found a raw milk source, chances are you've found a beef source! Dairy farmers often have 'down cows' (ones with banged up knees or other issues that don't affect the meat) that are sent to the butchers and are more than willing to sell a portion of them.

"And if you buy direct from the farmer? You'll usually get to pick your cuts and they will be at an incredible discount. Ground beef is cheap, but it can cost very little to add in a few fancy cuts to your order. Check the prices and you may be surprised.

"And don't forget the 'extras' from the cow… you can get liver, heart and other things for little-to-nothing. And the wonderful people at our butcher shop are more than willing to run my tallow through a grinder, making it easier for me to render. I think they charge me $5 for that service—well worth it!"

–Natasha

"I've loved the few times we've bought a large portion of a cow. I think we split half a cow with my brother-in-law's girlfriend's mother! I like the convenience of having so much beef on hand. It's one less thing to worry about buying every few weeks."

–Claire

"Another choice is venison. I have a freezer full of ground deer, cubed deer, deer stew, etc. My parents have hunting land, and supply us with three deer each year. We take it to be processed into packaged cuts of meat, tenderized and ready to cook. It is possible to go all year without buying ground beef with this kind of blessing. It works for meatloaf, salisbury steaks, chili, cheeseburger soup, burgers, enchiladas, tacos, tenderloin steaks for breakfast, cubed steaks and stew meat for dinner.

"It is lean and ideal, straight from nature to the table. Of course, it would depend on your area, availability, or laws regarding hunting wildlife, I suppose. Say…you might spend $150 or $200 a year for processing, leaving the need to buy chicken and fish only. I actually prefer the taste of venison now. And I am thankful that I don't have to participate in the hunt or processing."

–Stacie

Stepping Stones
to Better Meat Choices

- Find a butcher offering fresh beef and get a portion for dinner this week.

- Make a batch of seasoned hamburgers from scratch and experience the flavor and cost difference!

- Buy a whole chicken and try your hand at cutting it into parts. (Look it up on YouTube if you're not sure where to start!)

- Find the nearest source of pasture-raised chickens. Call or visit the farm to learn when and how you can get a discount on their birds.

- Discover which of your friends would split a quarter of a cow or a bulk order of pastured chickens with you.

Final Destination

All your meat is sourced from animals raised in a clean, healthy environment, eating what they were designed to eat, free of antibiotics and GMO feed.

Cheeseburger Soup (pg. 81)—Cordito (pg. 49)

Enjoying Bone Broth Every Day

Introducing a real food superstar you can make while you sleep!

I love bone broth! I love it because it's:

- super good for you,
- very inexpensive (okay, it's practically free),
- simple to make,
- super flavorful,
- easy to feed to my family.

Even when life is hectic, even when we're living on our converted bus, even in the heat of summer, bone broth is a constant in my kitchen. First I'll tell you how to make bone broth, then where to sneak it in so you get some of this goodness in your meals every day!

How to Make Chicken Bone Broth

Next time you debone or roast a chicken and have a pile of bones left over...

Step 1: Add ingredients

Throw the bones into your Crockpot (or a large stock pot on the stove), and add water up to the brim. Add a few tablespoons of vinegar or lemon juice to help draw out the goodness in the bones.

Step 2: Cook

Simmer the broth on low for at least eight hours—I usually start mine after dinner so it cooks all night. It's important that the bones simply simmer because boiling them can make the stock have a very strong, rather unpleasant flavor.

Step 3: Strain and store

In the morning, strain stock through a colander and divide between glass jars (leave two inches of head-space if freezing). Cap and cool completely before moving to fridge or freezer for later use. In the fridge, stock will usually last seven to ten days (you can tell when it's gone bad—it will smell rotten). You can also pour stock into ice cube trays and later store the frozen stock cubes in Ziploc bags for quick additions to sauces or smoothies.

Now, you can absolutely get all fancy and throw in veggies and garlic and spices, and you can skim the fat for use elsewhere, and you can condense it for fuller flavor or to conserve space in the freezer, and I've done all of that. But this basic technique is easy enough for me to get done even in busy seasons. With a recipe this simple, I'm rarely without broth on hand, and I use it frequently to increase nutrition in the meals I serve. Here's what I use broth for every day:

Ten Ways to Enjoy Broth Every Day

1. Cook pasta in it (replace about half the water with chicken broth).
2. Cook rice in it (replace the water the recipe calls for with chicken broth).
3. Use it as a base for favorite soups (instead of a bouillon cube + water).
4. Sip a mug with your meal (aids digestion and the feeling of satiation).
5. Use it (in place of water) to dilute your baby's pureed veggies.
6. Use to moisten and add flavor to mashed potatoes.
7. Use in white sauces and cheese sauces if you run out of milk.
8. Make your own "Cream of {Whatever} Soup".
9. Dehydrate it to make your own bouillon.
10. Freeze it in ice cube trays and add just a few to your breakfast smoothie to get broth into your diet even on the hot days of summer (you don't taste the bone broth at all!).

Of course, the main thing I use bone broth for is soups—hello! We love both chili and cheeseburger soup (see chapter 13) and they just don't have the flavor or depth of nutrition without homemade bone broths.

Cream of {Whatever} Soup

This recipe makes just under five cups of soup, which you can use (without diluting further) in any recipe that calls for canned, creamed soups.

- ½ c. butter
- Optional: ½ c. finally diced onions, mushrooms, or celery
- ½ c. flour
- 2 c. chicken broth
- 2 c. milk
- 1 t. freshly ground pepper
- 1 t. salt
- ½ t. garlic powder
- 2 t. sucanat or sweetener of your choice

Melt the butter in a two quart or larger saucepan, and add whatever diced vegetables you like and cook until soft. (If you're not adding any vegetables, just melt the butter). Whisk in the flour and cook about a minute, until bubbly but not brown. Gradually add first the chicken stock, then the milk, and then the rest of the seasonings. Cook until thick and bubbly.

Stepping Stones

for Making Broth a Daily Habit

- Buy your next chicken with the bone in.
- Make a batch of broth and freeze it as ice cubes.
- Try one of the soup recipes in this book.
- Next time you make a smoothie, throw a few stock cubes in.

Final Destination

Enjoy the benefits of homemade bone broth on a daily basis.

Sloppy Joes (pg. 86)—Soaked Rolls (pg. 87)

Reducing Grains and Preparing Them Wisely

Grains have gotten a bad rap in recent years. They're blamed for everything from our belly fat to allergies, and many people have ditched them entirely. I'm all for avoiding foods our bodies don't agree with, and I personally go on the grain-free GAPS diet one month each year just to give my digestive system a break and a boost. However, I believe that if we're preparing grains properly and eating them in moderation, we can benefit from having them in our diet.

{Note: If you are currently allergic to grains, I am not encouraging consumption of them until you have healed your gut. I highly recommend looking into the GAPS diet. This diet focuses on using nutritious bone broths and enzyme-rich cultured foods to heal a digestive tract that is sensitive to grains. It also addresses many other conditions such as neurological disorders, dairy intolerance, and seasonal allergies!}

Two Steps to Enjoying and Properly Preparing Grains

Step One: Moderation

We eat way too many grains these days, people! They are cheap, shelf-stable, and convenient in their packaged form so we default to them for too many snacks and main dishes. To avoid building intolerance to grains and to continue to enjoy them without the associated weight gain and health problems, we must learn to:

- Plan meals around veggies and protein instead of grain.
- Skip grain as a side dish–your meal can be complete and delicious without the rolls or garlic bread!
- Choose one meal a day or one day a week to go "grain free" and build your repertoire of recipes that don't rely on grain.
- Enjoy delicious desserts that are naturally grain free–fruits, crustless cheesecakes, and, of course, ice cream!

Step Two: Preparation

For thousands of years, from primitive people groups to gourmet bakers in Europe, grains have been soaked, sprouted, or fermented (think sourdough!) before baking. Only in the last century, have these slower, more nutritional approaches to grain preparation been abandoned in favor of convenience and profit margin. Proper grain preparation can be found in the three S's:

- Sprouting involves soaking the grain in water before it is ground, allowing it to start the germination process. Suddenly the grain's nutritional content skyrockets *and* it becomes easier to digest! After sprouting, the grain is dried and then ground into flour.

- Soaking can be done after a grain is already ground into flour. A pre-dough is made with the flour and some acidic liquid such as kefir, yogurt, buttermilk, whey or even lemon juice. This is left at room temperature for at least eight hours, then the rest of the ingredients are added and the baking process continues as normal. Soaking begins to break down the elements of the grain that are difficult to digest, and also produces a lighter whole-grain loaf.

- Sourdough is the traditional method of preparing grains that also uses natural yeast as leavening. It's probably the trickiest technique of the three S's, but well worth mastering for the variety of delicious breads and snacks you can make. I experimented with sourdough for the first time last year, and was delighted to find that I could use my starter to make everything from waffles to donuts to tortillas!

Soaking and Sprouting: Not Just for Grains!

Any food that is a seed–from beans and nuts to all types of grains–can benefit from soaking or sprouting. Dry beans should be soaked overnight and rinsed before cooking. Nuts should be soaked in salt water overnight (one tablespoon salt per four cups of nuts with enough water to cover) and dried in a dehydrator or oven on low before snacking on or baking with them. Maybe you've used nuts as a replacement for junk food snacks, and that's great, but nuts contain lots of enzyme inhibitors so you're doing your digestion a favor if you learn to soak them first.

How to Make Sprouted Wheat Flour:

"How in the world do you sprout flour?" is a question I often get from people screwing up their faces, trying to understand how you perform such a feat. If you've never done it, or seen the process, sprouted flour can seem mysterious and intimidating. The answer is simple though: you don't sprout the flour, you sprout the grain, dehydrate it, then grind it into flour. Here's the process as I do it in my own kitchen:

- **Step One: Soaking**
  Fill a quart or half gallon jar half full with wheat kernels. Fill the jar to the top with water. Let soak on the counter for 12 hours.

- **Step Two: Sprouting**
  Drain the water off the grains (either through a sprouting lid or using a colander), then let the grain sit in the jar for another 12-24 hours until it starts to sprout. Run water over the grains and drain them every few hours or as often as needed to keep them damp. Watch for signs that the grain has begun sprouting.

- **Step Three: Drying**
  When the grain has started to sprout (a little, white point poking out of one end of the kernel), it's time to dry it. Use a dehydrator if you have one, if not there are plenty of other ways to dry

the grain: cover a kitchen rack with a non-terry cloth kitchen towel or a pillowcase, or find an old screen and wash it. Spread the grain out on your improvised dehydrator and place it in the oven on warm, in the sun, or over a heat vent in your house in the winter.

- **Step Four: Grinding**
When the grain has dried (usually takes about 4-18 hours, depending on your drying method), grind it just as you would regular grain. The resulting flour has a slightly different texture and flavor, but has a much higher boost of nutrients and is more easily digested. I use sprouted wheat flour by itself or mixed with unbleached white flour in everything from cookies to pasta to sandwich bread to add nutrition and lighten the digestive burden.

If you have a mild sensitivity to wheat products, sprouted wheat may be a great option for you. My nephew's asthma is triggered by too much wheat in his diet. But when his mom makes sprouted wheat for him, he can enjoy cookies and breads without a reaction!

(Don't have a grain mill? Check out the tips in chapter 15)

How to Soak Whole Wheat Dough

There is some question in real food circles whether soaking dough is really that beneficial. Some say it helps break down the enzyme inhibitors naturally found in nuts and seeds, some say it isn't necessary. I'm no scientist and I'm not going to spend time debating just how good it is. I just know it's not bad for you, and when I soak my bread dough and muffin batter before baking, it results in a fluffier, lighter texture than my previous experiences with whole wheat baked goods. So, I soak whenever a recipe is conducive to it. Here's the basic method—if you want to try it yourself, the recipe section contains muffins, pancakes, cornbread, and yeast rolls that all have soaking instructions built into the recipe!

Mix the majority of the whole wheat flour your recipe calls for with an acid medium (yogurt, kefir, whey, buttermilk or even vinegar if you can't do dairy—2 T. per cup of flour) and enough other liquid (milk or water) to make a moist dough. Cover and leave on the counter at least eight hours or overnight to allow the dough to begin to ferment. In the morning or when you're ready to bake, mix in the rest of your ingredients and beat or knead until it's incorporated into your soaked dough. Often you have to add a bit more flour to get the dough the right consistency. This flour will not receive the benefits of soaking, so I use unbleached white flour which has had the difficult-to-digest bran and germ already removed. I am comfortable with the minimal presence of some white flour in my baked goods, but if you are trying for 100% soaked or sprouted grains, you could use sprouted wheat flour to adjust your dough instead. Once dough has reached the desired consistency, continue the recipe as usual.

Stepping Stones

for Reducing and Preparing Grains Properly:

- Plan one meal or an entire day this week to be grain free at your house.
- Try one of the soaked dough recipes from the recipe section of this book. (The muffins are the easiest!)
- Find a source for whole wheat kernels so you can experiment with sprouting or grinding your own.

Final Destination

Grains move from center stage to a supporting role in your diet, and you soak, sprout, or otherwise prepare your grains in a manner that makes them easier to digest.

Oven-Baked Pancake (pg. 68)

Choosing Natural Sweets and Enjoying Them Wisely

Let's be honest—sweets are the one area most of us are willing to fudge a bit on (pun intended). We all know sugar isn't a blessing to our bodies, but it's hard to give it up. The good news is there are a lot of choices we can make that are better for our bodies without having to say goodbye to our sweet tooth entirely.

The goal in this step is to lessen the negative impact of sugar in our diet, and we're going to do that by consuming it less, and making sure we choose well when we do have desserts.

The first step to reducing sugar intake is to reduce cravings. There's a reason the chapter on sweets is toward the end of the ten key steps, and that's because it's a lot easier to reduce sugar cravings when your body's nutritional needs are being met. I've seen a pattern in our family: when I'm on the top of my game and our diet is deeply nourishing, we don't crave sweets. But when I slack off or life gets interrupted, we suddenly can't get our minds off a sugar fix. This is most apparent whenever we've been without raw milk for awhile and my husband and I both start to crave junk food. I shared in Chapter 3 how upping my fat intake is what allowed me to finally break my carb addiction. So, the first step is to fill up on good fats and proteins.

Next, we need to rethink the place of sugar in our lives. In the standard American diet, sugar factors into every meal. But sugar should be used for celebrations, not as daily fuel. While my family quite regularly consumes fruit and naturally sweet vegetables like sweet potatoes, and we enjoy honey or maple syrup with oatmeal and pancakes, we do not eat dessert after every meal, and concoctions such as pie or cake are reserved for special occasions.

Choosing natural sweeteners is another key step. White sugar is made from the juice of sugar beets, sugar cane, or corn, but it is so refined that none of the good stuff like B vitamins and magnesium are left. Corn syrup, high fructose corn syrup, and brown sugar all fall in this category (brown sugar is simply bleached white sugar with some molasses added back in for coloring). Stripped of naturally occurring nutrients, refined sugars deliver short-term energy to our systems without any of the benefits of the enzymes or minerals found in natural sweeteners. Natural, minimally refined sweeteners like raw honey, pure maple syrup, and dehydrated cane juice (a dry form of naturally brown sugar sold as Sucanat or Rapadura) should be our choice because of the vitamins and minerals they can deliver to our systems while we enjoy them.

Finally, we need to enjoy sweeteners in the presence of other whole foods to lessen their negative impact on our system. Whether you eat a slice of apple or a piece of candy, the sugar in that treat immediately increases your blood glucose levels, and is followed swiftly by a an energy crash as insulin pumps into your system to restore balance. This blood sugar bungee jump is one of the most dangerous aspects of sugar intake because eventually these drastic ups and downs wear out your body's ability to process any form of sugar, leading to hypoglycemia, diabetes, and other blood sugar challenges. One of the ways to reduce the negative impact of sweets on our bodies, both in the short and long term, is to combine sweets with fats and proteins. The fats slow down digestion, letting the sugar enter our system at a more manageable rate, and the protein will provide fuel long after the sugar has been burned up, meaning steady energy levels throughout the day.

For this reason, I've made the effort to cultivate in my family an appreciation for full fat desserts such as cheesecake and homemade ice cream (it hasn't been hard!). We also eat dessert directly after a meal instead of waiting an hour or two and subjecting ourselves to a sugar bomb and subsequent coma. It's hard to over-indulge on sweets when your stomach is already full and the dessert is rich—that's the way it should be!

With these ideas and goals, it's been fairly easy to keep sugar to a minimum in our household. But then, just when you think you've conquered the cookie monster, along come the holidays!

How to Keep Your Real Foodie Badge During the Holidays

So many holiday traditions and family celebrations center around food, that this is an area of real challenge for even the most committed real foodie. I know I am not immune to the siren call of my in-laws' chocolate-covered peanut butter balls at Christmastime! It's hard to walk away from traditions that have been passed down for generations. My efforts over the years have involved substituting, experimenting, some guilt from indulgence, and then those moments of glory – when my naturally sweetened creation comes close enough to tradition to satisfy. Here are four steps for a real food approach to the traditional holiday fare.

1. Find nourishing ingredients

Make your treats as good for you as possible. Use a natural form of sugar, rather than ultra-refined, bleached white sugar. Use real butter instead of Crisco or margarine (trust me, this does not negatively affect most recipes!). Use dark cocoa and quality chocolate. Shop local for fresher, more nourishing ingredients. Nuts and flours go rancid so quickly—find sources for the best quality you can afford. If it costs extra, it will be just one more reason not to overindulge! I use sucanat in all my baking, coconut oil and butter for fats, and avoid food coloring all together. Yes, my kids fussed at bit that our cut-out cookies weren't as colorful as the neighbor's, but it's been three years now and our albino Santas and Christmas trees have become the new tradition.

2. Bake cookies

I'm serious—just deciding not to make cookies yourself means you will be in complete withdrawal and subject to uncontrollable cravings when you visit others or receive plates of cookies from friends! Make your own treats so you can have something yummy along with everyone else. Don't be ashamed to bring your own healthier creations to the Christmas party, even if it's a little different than the other choices on the buffet. You're doing what's right for *your* family.

3. Exercise moderation

Just because there are piles and stacks and bins of cookies all around you does not mean that *you* have to be the one to keep them from going stale! Decide ahead of time what your favorite treats are, and what forms of sugar just aren't worth it (for me, it's chocolate instead of candy every time!). Limit yourself to one treat a day. Savor it. And share your goodies with others so you don't have so much lying around!

4. Save the sugar for dessert

Try to keep sugar to a minimum in the other meals you make. Choose savory over sweet for your breakfast menus. The Christmas breakfast of my childhood was sweet rolls or coffee cake. I have added a hearty, grain-free egg casserole to the menu, and soak my coffee cake dough overnight. I make lots of savory breakfasts and batches of oatmeal during December to balance out the indulgences that we have at parties.

Sugar puts a strain on our bodies and weakens your immune system. So often, when I overindulge on sugar, I can feel it – either a general sluggishness, or succumbing to a head cold when it's the least convenient. Keep your family happy and healthy by nourishing them with good cooking between all the sweet treats, and make sure the goodies you make are as nourishing as possible.

Stepping Stones

for A Naturally Sweet Lifestyle

- Commit to making cookies and cakes from scratch rather than buying them.
- Find a source for local, raw honey, and learn to use it in baking.
- Switch from bleached white sugar to mineral-rich alternatives like sucanat.
- Build your repertoire of fruit-sweetened, low-sugar desserts.
- Adjust your family favorites to be made with full fat ingredients.
- Eat sweets in conjunction with a meal or protein.

Final Destination

You don't resort to sugar for quick fuel, but nourish your body with real food, and use natural sweeteners for celebrations.

Left to right
Kimchi (pg. 50)
Cordito (pg. 49)
German Sauerkraut (pg. 51)
Gingered Carrots (pg. 48)

Get Cultured with Fermented Foods

Enzymes are a key ingredient in a nourishing diet, allowing us to properly digest the food we're eating and get the most nutrients out of it. Our intestines do not actually digest our food—they simply provide housing for millions of tiny organisms that do the work of breaking our food down into nutrients our body can use. If we are deficient in good bacteria and essential enzymes, we won't get the full benefit from all this good food we've been cooking!

Enzymes are easy to find—they're in all raw food. But a plate of salad contains only enough enzymes to digest that salad. So how do you get enough enzymes to digest a meal that is mostly cooked? The answer comes in adding fermented and cultured foods to our daily menu.

When you culture or ferment food, the good bacteria and enzyme count skyrockets, meaning you can eat a tablespoon of a fermented condiment with your meal, and it is sufficient to digest the whole plate!

I took a digestive enzyme supplement regularly the first six years of my real food journey. I hated taking expensive pills, but my body needed support in this area (as most of us do). But gradually, as I learned to make and add cultured condiments and drinks to my diet, I've been able to wean myself off the supplement with no reoccurrence of digestive issues!

Learning to love sauerkraut was a journey for me, people. I don't naturally like anything with a vinegary or pickled flavor. But just a little exploring into this area of real food led to some delightful discoveries that have helped me make sauerkraut a part of my lifestyle.

In this chapter, I'm going to walk you through the fermented condiments we eat at our house. Notice I said condiments—that's the key to enjoying this stuff. It's not a side dish, so don't feel guilty if you can only stand a small spoonful mixed into your meal, because *that's exactly how it's done.*

Another key to actually enjoying fermented vegetables is variety. There are actually several different kinds of sauerkraut and many types of fermented vegetables, and each pairs better with certain dishes, *kind of like different wines*. I'm going to share the different types we've tried at our house, and the foods we enjoy them with. Don't feel like you need to make all of these this month—the broad selection is meant to give you variety to choose from, not overwhelm you.

Basic Method for Fermenting Vegetables

First, we'll talk about method. It's not a complicated process, but it does involve getting the right balance of good bacteria and there may be a bit of a learning curve for you, as there was for me (I tried making traditional German sauerkraut three times before I got a successful batch). But I will tell you–cabbage and labor are cheap. If you fail, try again. It's not that hard.

The basic method for fermenting vegetables goes like this:

1. Chop or grate the veggies finely (though not so finely as to create pulp)
2. Mix in some salt
3. Pound it until it's bruised and juicy
4. Pack tightly into a jar
5. Pour a little whey or reserved juice from your last batch of kraut over the top
6. Cap and leave on counter for a few days to ferment
7. Refrigerate and enjoy

How will you know if it doesn't turn out? This is the part I'm an expert about! It'll mold, turn pink, smell putrid, or all of the above. Trust me–*you'll know*. Throw it out and try again. No big deal. I repeat: cabbage and labor are cheap.

To enjoy your fermented condiments, add them after you've put your food on your plate—cooking them destroys all the good reasons you're eating them!

Gingered Carrots

Gingered carrots are one of the simplest fermented vegetables to make and incorporate into your menu. The carrots' natural sweetness help overcome the vinegary flavor of most fermented veggies, and it pairs nicely with many familiar dishes. Makes about one quart.

- 4 c. grated carrots
- 1 T. fresh grated ginger
- 1 T. sea salt
- 4 T. whey or reserved liquid from another batch of fermented veggies

Mix all ingredients in a large bowl and pound with a meat hammer or the bottom of a quart jar for about five minutes to release juices. Pack the carrots into a quart-sized, wide-mouthed Mason jar and tamp down until juices cover the carrots. The top of the carrots should be at least one inch below the top of the jar. Cover tightly and leave at room temperature for three days before storing in fridge. Keeps for months, but it should be tossed if it grows pretty colors of mold, or tastes or smells horrid.

I serve gingered carrots on stir-fry (added after it's done cooking and cooled sufficiently so as not to kill the enzymes), tossed into a salad with my favorite berry vinaigrette, a few tablespoons stirred into carrot-raisin-pineapple salad, and as a condiment when I make baked stuffed chicken breasts. It adds lovely color to a plate, and really doesn't taste like sauerkraut at all.

I've even made Gingered Carrots while traveling on our family bus, which shows that even with a small kitchen and limited resources, you can fit this into your lifestyle!

Cordito (Mexican Sauerkraut)

I vote cordito to be the easiest sauerkraut to add to your menu. It's Mexican in origin, made with carrots, onions and cabbage and seasoned with oregano and red pepper. You just throw it on with the salsa, sour cream, olives, and other toppings you're layering in your taco, and then enjoy the subtle-yet-incredibly-authentic flavor it adds to every bite.

I can't believe I just basically wrote an ode to sauerkraut. But I'm not lying, people. This really is another painless experience in adding lacto-fermented condiments into your diet. Makes 2-3 pints.

- 1 large cabbage, cored and shredded
- 1 c. grated carrots
- 2 medium onions, quartered lengthwise and very finely sliced
- 1 T. dried oregano
- ¼-½ t. red pepper flakes
- 1 T. sea salt
- 4 T. whey or "juice" from another batch of kraut

Mix all together in a large bowl, pound for 5-10 minutes to release juices, then transfer to glass jars, tamping down kraut till juices rise above the surface of the cabbage. You should leave one inch of headspace between cabbage and top of jar. Cap and leave on counter three days, then transfer to fridge.

Here's my favorite thing about cordito – it blends in so well with the many other toppings on a taco or things you toss in a taco salad, that *I've actually got my husband and kids to eat this one.* When we have taco salad as a family, I've taken to tossing the lettuce, meat, cheese, and crushed chips in a bowl with most of the toppings, then let my husband add more hot salsa to his serving if he wants it. This means simpler serving for the kids and lots less fuss for Mom. A few tablespoons of cordito are hardly noticed amongst spoonfuls of sour cream and salsa, and down the hatch it goes.

Kimchi {Korean Sauerkraut}

I first met kimchi when I was on the GAPS diet. It was a great experience in fermented veggies as it seemed to fit very closely into the "salsa" category for me. It's colorful, spicy, and very versatile. Makes 2-3 pints.

- 1 head cabbage, Napa or regular, quartered and shredded
- 1 bunch green onions, chopped
- 1 c. grated carrots
- ½ c. grated daikon radishes, optional
- 1 T. freshly grated ginger
- 3 cloves garlic, chopped fine
- ½ t. dried chili flakes
- 1 T. sea salt
- 4 T. whey

Mix all together in a large bowl, pound for 5-10 minutes to release juices, then transfer to glass jars, tamping down kraut till juices rise to the surface. Cap and leave on counter for three days, then transfer to fridge.

I first used kimchi in GAPS soups–an otherwise simple broth, veggie, and meat puree was taken up a notch with the addition of a tablespoon of just the juice from a jar of kimchi. Later in the diet, I put the veggies themselves in the soup, adding a delightful bit of texture to my meal. One morning I even had it with my breakfast of steak, eggs, and avocado. I never thought I'd have sauerkraut with breakfast, but my mouth is actually watering as I write this. *This is so weird.*

Anyway, kimchi taught me another easy way to enjoy sauerkraut: a spoonful in any kind of soup just like–or even alongside–that dollop of sour cream, sprinkle of cheese, or handful of crushed crackers. Just make sure your soup has cooled to your tongue before you add it—if it will burn your tongue, it will effectively cook the goodness right out of your sauerkraut.

Her Royal Majesty, Queen of Sauerkrauts

Finally, we meet the Queen of Sauerkraut: traditional German kraut. This is the form of sauerkraut that most of us have at least a slight acquaintance with, though often it is bought from the store in a can which means it's been cooked and is missing the very ingredient that makes sauerkraut the superfood that it is: enzymes. Don't settle for the limp, dead kraut that comes in a can. Learn to make your own traditional kraut to enjoy with classic, European favorites like meat, potatoes, and stew.

You can make it with or without caraway seeds, and if you choose a purple cabbage (which I totally recommend) you get a regal purple condiment to add to your favorite meat and potatoes meal. Makes about 1 ½ - 2 quarts, depending on the size of your cabbage.

- 1 medium cabbage, cored and shredded
- 1 T. caraway seeds (optional)
- 1 T. sea salt
- 4 T. whey

In a bowl, mix cabbage with (optional) caraway seeds, sea salt, and whey. Pound with a wooden pestle (or the bottom of a quart jar) for about ten minutes to release juices. Place in a quart-sized, wide-mouth Mason jar and press down firmly until juices come to the top of the cabbage. You should have one inch of space between the cabbage and the top of the jar. Cover tightly and keep at room temperature for about three days before storing it in the fridge. You can eat it right away, but it improves with age. Oh, and it keeps eons in the fridge...I literally had a jar that was better than ever after sitting in the back of my fridge for over a year!

I find traditional German sauerkraut to be perfect for meat and potatoes, beef stew, and any savory winter meal. I personally think that even if you're not Dutch (like I am) or German, you can learn to enjoy sauerkraut with your meat and potatoes. My husband feels differently and gives me funny looks whenever I turn my potatoes pink with a spoonful of purple kraut, but lately my three-year-old and five-year-old have been asking for a scoop because they think pink potatoes are fun! I'll admit that I'm not always in the mood for the extra flavor (or the trouble of fetching a condiment out of the fridge when I might be the only one interested in using it), but it remains a simple, cheap way to boost the nutritional value of a meal.

Lacto-Fermented Salsa

If you've ever made fresh salsa before, you're just one step away from this delicious summer favorite. And, if your garden has been fruitful, but you're not in the mood to can salsa, take heart. The fermenting this salsa undergoes helps it last weeks in the fridge, so you can skip the canning! Makes about a quart.

- 4 medium tomatoes, peeled and diced
- 2 small onions (or one large), chopped
- ¾ c. chopped peppers, any combination of sweet or spicy
- 6-8 cloves garlic, crushed
- 1 bunch fresh cilantro (chopped to equal about a cup)
- Juice of 2 lemons
- 1 T. sea salt
- 4 T. whey

Combine all ingredients in a large bowl and portion into wide-mouthed mason jars. Press down tightly to bring juices over the top of the vegetables, adding a bit of water if necessary to have enough liquid. Cover tightly and keep on counter at room temperature for 2 days, then transfer to the fridge. Use just as you would regular salsa!

Cultured Refried Beans

A unique, lacto-fermented condiment that will change your chip's life! Makes about a pint.

- 1 ½ c. cooked beans (kidney or pinto are tasty)
- ¼ of a whole onion, chunked
- 1-2 cloves garlic, peeled
- 1 t. salt
- 2 T. whey

Combine all in a blender and process till smooth. Pour into a pint jar (or two smaller jelly jars), leaving one inch of head space between beans and top of jar. Screw lid(s) on tightly and leave on counter at room temperature for three days. Transfer to fridge. Keeps several months.

Use as a dip for veggies or quesadillas, dab onto top of enchiladas or tacos, or toss into a taco salad.

(Find instructions for soaking and cooking your own beans with the chili recipe on pg. 82)

Lacto-Fermented Mayonnaise

Making your own mayonaise from scratch means you get to choose high-quality ingredients, and you can lacto-ferment it, which gives you a super-beneficial condiment to use with favorite meals like hamburgers! Suddenly your mayonnaise goes from a shady character with evil intentions toward your gallbladder, to an enzyme-rich, deeply nourishing companion which will aid digestion and boost the nutrition of any meal you serve it with. Makes just over a cup of mayonnaise, which will keep for up to two months.

- 1 egg
- 1 egg yolk
- 1 T. lemon juice
- 1 T. whey (see Chapter 4)
- ¼ t. salt
- ¼ t. pepper
- 1 t. brown mustard or ½ t. dry mustard powder
- 1 c. of good fats

It's best if you work with room temperature eggs, so the day you plan to make mayo, set some eggs on the counter first thing in the morning.

I use a mixture of oils in my mayonnaise because I don't like to it to come out too strongly flavored by an individual oil. My typical proportions are ⅓ c. olive oil, ⅓ c. coconut oil, and ⅓ c. sesame or sunflower or whatever other mild-flavored oil I have on hand. The coconut oil can be lightly heated to allow you to pour and mix it easily with the other ingredients.

Measure the first seven ingredients into your blender and add enough of your oil (about ⅓ c.) to bring the contents up to the height of the mixing blades. Blend ingredients on medium speed and then begin adding the rest of your oil in a thin, slow stream. It should take you 3-5 minutes to gradually add the remaining ⅔ c. of oil. By the time you have added the last of the oil, the mixture should have emulsified and thickened. (If it turns out more runny, don't worry—it will thicken some in the fridge, and even a "failed" batch of mayo still works great for salad dressing.) Scoop mayo into a glass jar, cap it, and leave it on the counter for seven hours to allow the lacto-fermentation time to work. Then transfer your mayo to the fridge.

If you don't have whey or are planning to use the mayonnaise immediately in a recipe, you can skip the fermentation on the counter and just store the mayonnaise in the fridge until you're ready to use it. Keep in mind that lacto-fermented mayonnaise will last several months in the fridge, but without whey, your mayonnaise will be good for only a week.

Water Kefir

Water kefir, or kefir soda, is simple, cultured drink that can aid digestion. Although it's ridiculously easy to make, I don't consider myself to be an expert so I asked my friend Gretchen to give you the scoop. (We're all on different parts of the journey, even me!) Don't let all the details intimidate you—when it comes down to it, kefir takes about five minutes to make and is a healthy alternative to soda!

Gretchen says...

There are many methods and variations of water kefir but here's a basic, easy to remember method of culturing a delicious probiotic your whole family will enjoy. The only ingredient you might not have in your kitchen is the kefir grains. Just ask around, you'll be surprised how many people are willing to share. Or, order your own from an online source like Cultures for Health.

First Ferment

- ⅓ c. water kefir grains
- ⅓ c. sugar
- 1 quart water

In a quart jar, dissolve sugar in a small amount of warm water. Then fill the rest of the jar to two inches below the rim with cold water. Add kefir grains and cover securely with cheesecloth or a cloth napkin (use a rubber band to hold the cloth in place). Let sit for 24-48 hours in a warm place, away from direct sunlight.

You can strain the kefir water from the grains and enjoy it immediately after the first ferment. Or you can ferment it a second time to add flavor and carbonation. This is the step that makes it like soda.

Second Ferment Carbonation Options

- 3 T. fresh fruit, slightly smashed
- 3 T. dried fruit (raisins, elderberry, etc.)
- ½ to 1 c. fruit juice

Second Ferment Flavor Ideas

- Raw or crystalized ginger
- Citrus slices or peels
- 2-3 t. vanilla extract
- Whole caraway, anise, or fennel seed
- Fresh mint leaves

Strain kefir water from your first ferment into a new quart jar (save the grains for another batch). Now, add a source of fructose (fruit sugar) to simultaneously feed and carbonate the kefir (you'll only need one of the fruit source measurements listed above). Also, add any combination of flavors (the ideas above are just a few suggestions).

Secure lid loosely and leave it to ferment for an additional 24-48 hours. (You'll know it's working if, after a few hours, bubbles rise when you tip the jar slightly.) Enjoy over ice, or refrigerate for up to two weeks for future use.

Dos & Don'ts in Kefir Grain Care:

- Do use un-chlorinated, un-fluoridated, un-distilled water.

- Don't add kefir grains to hot water (room temperature is best).

- Don't use metal containers or utensils.

- Do use unrefined, raw sugar (with the molasses still intact) like Sucanat or Rapadura for best results. If using white or brown sugar, add ⅓ t. organic blackstrap molasses with each ⅓ c. sugar.

- Don't use raw honey (the antibacterial properties in honey will fight with the good bacteria in the kefir).

- Do use a fructose sugar source in the second culture.

- Do change out fruit every 24 hours during the unrefrigerated part of the second culture (so the kefir has something to feed on).

- Do store in glass (or food-grade plastic).

- Do brew away from direct sunlight.

Notes

Second Ferment: The second fermentation process does produce some alcohol that varies with each batch; but, according to most sources, it's less than 1%, which is less than naturally occurs in ripe fruit. But if you don't want the fizziness or any alcohol, you can enjoy all the probiotic benefits of kefir water by drinking it after the first ferment Just add some fruit juice or maple syrup for flavor right before you drink it, or mix it with a smoothie.

Ratios: It's easy to remember the right ratios if you remember the rule of 3s: ⅓ c. kefir grains, ⅓ c. sugar, 32 ounces water (1 quart). For the second culture, it's 3 T. fruit to every 32 ounces of kefir water.

Fermenting: You'll know the probiotic culture has worked if the water changes color throughout the first ferment and if it develops bubbles throughout the second ferment. The flavor should change from sugar water to a slight yeast/vinegar taste after the first ferment, with the first fermented kefir being less sweet than the sugar water. If anything else starts growing in your kefir (mold, bugs), or it smells differently than normal, ask an experienced friend for help or contact the customer support at CulturesforHealth.com.

Grains: Healthy kefir grains multiply quite rapidly. Share the bounty with friends, toss a few in smoothies (go easy—they are super rich in yeast and good bacteria), or add them to your compost. A quick Google search reveals dozens of creative ways to use leftover kefir grains.

Rest: If you're traveling or otherwise need a break from making kefir, add enough water to cover your grains, add the sugar, secure the top with a lid, and put them in the refrigerator. Rinse and feed with fresh sugar water every few weeks.

Kefir soda was one of the first steps on my real food journey. When my son started having digestive issues, everyone recommend probiotics. The price of pills was outrageous, but then I heard about kefir soda: a delicious probiotic I could make at home. It's become my favorite drink, summer and winter. Kefir soda is a great alternative when I'm craving something a little sweet, and it helps settle the stomach when I eat something that doesn't agree with me. Who needs corn syrup laden soda pop when you can make your own healthy kefir soda at home? —Gretchen

Find more kefir information and inspiration at gretchenlouise.com/kefir/

Enzyme-Rich Lemonade

Here's another simple (and sweet!) way to add enzymes to a meal: a lemonade that's lacto-fermented! Makes nearly one gallon.

- ¾ c. lemon juice
- ½ to 1 c. sucanat (depending on if you like it sweet or tart)
- ¾ c. whey
- 3 quarts water

Mix everything in a gallon glass jar or large, glass bowl and let sit for two days at room temperature, then refrigerate and enjoy! Adding a little seltzer water can give it a nice fizz.

Stepping Stones

to Getting Cultured Foods into Your Menu

- Choose one of the recipes in this section to try this week.
- Try a new recipe every month until you have a variety of fermented condiments in your fridge.
- Learn to put a tablespoon of kraut or just the juice into bowls of soup when you serve it.
- Pull out the kimchi when you have a savory breakfast.
- Add gingered carrots or kimchi to your favorite salads.
- Let Mexican night be rich in enzymes by serving lacto-fermented salsa, cordito, cultured refried beans, or all the above!

Final Destination

To incorporate something cultured or fermented into every meal. For us, this goal looks like:

- A bit of yogurt or kefir with breakfast – usually in the form of a smoothie.
- A cultured or fermented drink with lunch.
- Cultured condiments like sauerkraut or lacto-fermented mayonnaise with dinner.

Learn the Art of Bulk Food Preparation

I know what you're thinking just about now—"How do you have time to cook so much from scratch?"

Well, let's see. I don't have TV, so that frees up a lot of my time…but I do have a smartphone, so there's always something to distract me from what I should be doing. It all comes down to priorities. I love the satisfaction of serving my family real food. I love that we feel strong, sleep well, and have robust immune systems. So I've come up with all kinds of tricks and strategies to reduce time and effort in the kitchen. I menu plan and think ahead and do a little advance prep for the next meal every time I'm in the kitchen. And? I practice the art of bulk food preparation.

Bulk cooking simply means you prepare more ingredients or food than you need for one meal so you have the makings of another meal in the future. There are three key ways to embrace bulk cooking:

Cook once, eat twice

This is a great habit to form in the real food kitchen—cooking double the amount your family will eat for that meal and freezing it. I use this method when I make casseroles because I do so love having a casserole or two in the freezer for busy days, but don't actually have the time in my schedule for a whole day devoted to freezer cooking. Doubling just one meal is doable. I'll be doing this tonight as I plan on making beef stroganoff for dinner. All it takes is thawing two packages of meat instead of one and chopping a bit more garlic, and I will have a second meal's worth of the gravy. Next week when I have a busy day, dinner will be as simple as thawing and reheating.

Prepare bulk meal components

If there's a meal component you use a lot in your kitchen, like beans, rice, or chicken stock, make as big a batch as possible and freeze individual, meal-sized portions for later use. When you've gotten away from over-processed, store-bought ingredients like cream of chicken soup, Hamburger Helper, or bouillon cubes, you miss the ability to quickly throw together a meal unless you bulk prepare parts of future dishes. I also grate cheese and make tortillas and pizza dough in large batches, freezing what we don't have immediate use for.

Make your own seasoning mixes

Another key way to save time when you make meals from scratch is to make your own seasoning mixes. If you have learned to skip the store-bought salad dressing or taco seasoning packages laced with MSG and too much sugar, you've made great progress, but the measuring of a half a dozen spices each time you cook that favorite meal can get tedious. Mix up bulk batches of your favorite seasoning combinations to make that step in your dinner preparation a breeze. Here are some of my favorites:

Taco Seasoning

- ½ c. dried onion
- ¼ c. sea salt
- ¼ c. chili powder
- ¼. c. arrowroot powder or organic cornstarch
- ¼ c. red pepper flakes
- ¼ c. garlic powder
- ¼ ground cumin
- 4 t. oregano
- 2 T. sucanat

Mix all ingredients and store in airtight container. To use, add 3 T. mix and ¼ c. water to one pound ground beef when browning.

Herbal Seasoned Salt

I use this seasoned salt (similar to Herbamare) in everything from soups to roast chicken to burgers.

- 1 c. sea salt
- 1 t. each of oregano, thyme, basil, dill, dried garlic, chives, sage, celery seed, and marjoram
- 2 t. dried onion powder
- ½ t. ground rosemary
- ½ c. parsley flakes

Measure all ingredients into your blender and pulse a few times to combine. Store in an airtight container and use in place of salt or as you would seasoned salt in your favorite recipes.

Healthy Valley Ranch Dressing Mix

- ¼ c. arrowroot powder
- ¼ c. sea salt
- ¼ c. garlic powder
- ¼ c. onion powder
- ½ c. parsley flakes
- 2 T. black pepper
- 1 t. dill
- 1 t. thyme
- 1 T. sucanat

To make dressing, combine 1 ½ t. mix with ¼ c. mayonnaise and ½ c. plain kefir or yogurt diluted with milk to buttermilk consistency. Whisk for a minute, store in fridge for up to a week.

Learning to cook quickly and efficiently is an important step to maintaining a real food lifestyle. But this too will take time. I've been on the journey for seven years now and have grown in my ability to fit real food into busy days. One new strategy, one new recipe, one new technique at a time—I practiced and it became part of our life. Learning to cook smarter, not harder, will help you avoid burnout and enjoy the journey.

For more tips on how to make real food faster, check out my first book, *Real {Fast} Food*. It's full of all my best tips for fitting real food prep like soaking and cooking and fermenting into your routine. It's also got over 60 real food recipes to add to your repertoire!

Stepping Stones

to an Efficient Real Food Kitchen

- When you go shopping next week, buy enough ingredients to make a double portion of a family favorite.
- Next time you make dinner, double it and freeze half.
- Try one of the seasoning mixes in this chapter.

Final Destination

Become a pro in your own kitchen, sometimes throwing dinner together as fast as with a boxed mix, and not letting even a busy schedule keep you from nutritious, homemade meals.

Tools for the Journey

Not Yo' Mama's Oatmeal (pg. 69)

Real Food Breakfast Champions

The real food day begins with a real food breakfast!

Three years ago, I wrote my first cookbook, *Real {Fast} Food*. It was based on several conversations I had with friends who expressed a desire to add more nourishing meals into their routine, but hesitated because of the time commitment they thought it would take. Each of these women truly didn't have any extra time in their day or week to put the effort into a healthier diet. They knew this. I knew this.

But I had an idea.

I figured if they would focus on just improving one meal a day in their diet, they could see a difference in their health goals and perhaps see enough results to make more changes. From talking to each of these women, I knew the meal they needed to focus on most was breakfast. They were starting their day with coffee and a quick muffin or bowl of cereal (if that), which set them up for low blood sugar and cravings for the rest of the day. So, I decided to coach them to start their day right, knowing a nourishing choice at breakfast would positively affect them all day. If they could find an hour a week, perhaps on the weekend, to do a little planning and batch cooking, they could manage to improve the quality of one third of their meals!

My one girlfriend really took my advice and ran with it. She began her real food journey by adding some protein (an omelet or nutrient-dense smoothie) to her morning routine, which previously had existed of only coffee or sometimes a sugary carb. Three years later, she has achieved every one of her health goals, including reaching her ideal body weight, overcoming some serious recurring health concerns, and feeling the energy she should as a 20-something. And it all started with breakfast!

So, here's a week's worth of real food breakfast ideas for you and your family. Make it your goal this week to start the day right. And remember that a good breakfast usually starts the night before, with a few minutes of planning or getting some grains to soak.

The Ultimate Breakfast Smoothie

We make this smoothie several times a week, varying what we add, but always including some good fats and egg yolks* for protein. When my husband quit coffee last year, he replaced it with this smoothie, and didn't suffer a single headache or craving. It really starts your day right. If you have an active lifestyle, are breastfeeding, or otherwise burning a lot of calories, I suggest pairing a smoothie with one of the other breakfast choices in this section. Serves 2.

- ½ c. fresh or frozen berries or other seasonal fruit
- 1 fresh or frozen banana
- 1 c. yogurt or kefir
- 1 T. maple syrup, honey, or frozen juice concentrate
- 2 egg yolks*
- 1 T. melted coconut oil
- 1 T. flax or chia seeds (optional)
- 1 handful fresh or steamed spinach, chard, or kale
- 4-6 ice cubes or frozen bone broth cubes

Combine all ingredients in blender and blend on high until smooth.

Play with the ingredients until you get a mix you love. My husband loves a pina colada smoothie with strawberries, banana, pineapple and some coconut milk thrown in. My kids love peanut butter and jelly smoothies with ½ c. peanut butter, a banana and lots of frozen berries. Keep your base full of good fats and proteins from the kefir, yogurt, and egg yolks, and you can throw just about anything in there!

*Raw egg yolks from healthy, pastured hens are similar to raw milk—full of vitamins and enzymes when eaten raw. If you know your farmer and the eggs are clean, you need not worry about the diseases common in eggs produced in concentrated animal feeding operations (CAFOs).

Chocolate Peanut Butter Muffins

You will love me when I tell you these are actually good for you. The grains soaking overnight make them more digestible, and the protein from the peanut butter and eggs makes this a well-rounded breakfast all on its own. Okay, you will want a tall glass of raw milk to wash it down!

Combine in a bowl:

- 1 c. oats
- 1 c. buttermilk, sour cream, yogurt, soured milk, or other acidic medium
- ½ c. peanut butter
- ½ c. whole wheat flour

Cover and let sit on counter overnight (or at least eight hours).

In a separate bowl, combine:

- ⅓ c. sprouted wheat flour OR white flour
- 1 t. baking powder
- ½ t. salt
- ½ t. baking soda

Set aside.

The next morning, preheat oven to 350°F, and grease (and line with paper cups if you have them) 12 muffin tins. Beat together

- 1 egg
- ½ c. sucanat, sugar, honey, or maple syrup
- ½ c. melted coconut oil or butter
- 1 t. vanilla

Stir this into the soaked oats and flour mixture.

Next add the flour and baking powder mixture to the bowl. Then fold in

- 1 c. chocolate chips
- 1 c. unsweetened coconut (optional)

Divide into 12 muffin cups and bake for 20 minutes. Makes 12 muffins.

Oven-Baked Pancake

One of our all-time favorites! So yummy topped with fresh, seasonal fruit. Serves 4.

- 2 c. whole wheat pastry flour
- 2 c. milk
- 6 T. butter (¾ stick)
- 3-4 eggs
- ½ t. almond extract or 1 t. vanilla extract
- ¼ t. salt
- 2 T. sucanat, or other form of sugar
- 1 c. berries or chopped fruit of your choice, optional

The night before, mix flour and milk together, cover, and let soak on counter overnight.

The next morning, preheat oven to 400°F. Slice the butter into chunks in a 9x13 pan and slide it right into the oven while it's preheating.

Meanwhile, mix the eggs, extract, and salt into the soaked flour. Add more milk until it's the consistency of pancake batter. When butter has melted into a puddle in your baking pan, pull it out of the oven. Pour batter into pan over top of butter, sprinkle with sucanat and berries, and slide back into the oven. Bake for 20-25 minutes until puffed and golden (and boy, does it puff – the kids will love this part!). Cut and serve in squares—easiest pancake breakfast ever!

Soaked Sour Cream Pancakes

As a teen, I used to quadruple this recipe to feed our family of nine! I remember going around all morning with the weight of a stack of pancakes in my middle. Soaking the flour overnight helps these pancakes sit lighter on the stomach and give you more nourishment from the grains.

- 3 c. flour
- ½ c. yogurt
- 1 c. milk
- 2 c. water
- ¼ c. butter, melted
- ½ c. sour cream
- 2 T. honey or sucanat
- 3 eggs
- 1 T. baking powder
- 1 t. salt

Mix flour with yogurt, milk, and water. Cover and leave on counter for at least eight hours or overnight. In the morning, stir in the melted butter, honey, sour cream, and then eggs. Mix into soaked flour and add more milk if necessary to get a normal pancake batter consistency. Finally, stir in baking powder and salt, and fry in butter or coconut oil.

Berry Delicious Baked Oatmeal

A handful of whatever berries you have—fresh or frozen—turns this simple make-ahead breakfast into something extra special. Makes 8-10 servings.

- 6 c. oats
- 2 c. water
- 2 c. yogurt or kefir
- 5-6 eggs
- ½ c. coconut oil or butter
- ½ c. honey, maple syrup, or sucanat
- 4 t. baking powder
- ½ t. baking soda
- ½ t. salt
- 2 t. cinnamon
- 1 c. fresh or frozen blueberries, strawberries, or berry of your choice.

The night before, combine oats, water, and yogurt or kefir. Cover and let soak on counter for at least eight hours or overnight. In the morning, preheat oven to 350°F and grease a 9x13 baking dish. Melt coconut oil or butter and add it and the rest of ingredients to the oat mixture and mix well. Pour into baking dish and bake for 45 minutes to one hour, until set in the middle. Serve with whole milk poured over the top!

Not Yo' Mama's Oatmeal

Maybe more like your grandma's, because it's soaked and full of good fats. This is my kids' all-time favorite breakfast and we often eat it 3-4 times a week. Serves 4.

- 2 c. rolled oats
- 3 c. water
- ¼ c. whey, yogurt, or kefir
- ½ t. salt
- ⅓ c. honey
- ½ – 1 t. cinnamon
- ½ c. raisins

Mix oats, water, and whey, yogurt or kefir together in a saucepan and let sit on the counter overnight. In the morning, put the pan on the stove on low, and bring to a simmer and cook until it's how you like it – thin and runny, or thick and gooey (sorry, there's just no nice way to describe this otherwise tasty dish!), about 15-20 minutes. Serve with a pat of butter and a bit of milk.

Mom Holden's Egg Casserole

I serve this with fresh fruit and coffee cake for a company breakfast, to rave reviews. Even kids like it because it is basically just scrambled eggs, and doesn't look foreign to them. I have also used crumbled breakfast sausage or diced ham in place of the bacon, or sometimes skip the meat altogether. The real beauty of this dish is how quickly it's ready in the morning. Serves 4-6.

- 1 dozen eggs
- ¼ c. milk
- ½ lb. bacon, cooked crisp, drained, and crumbled
- ½ c. sour cream
- 8 oz. grated cheddar cheese
- paprika, salt, and pepper to taste

Combine the eggs, milk, and salt and pepper and cook as for scrambled eggs. Transfer to a greased casserole dish (I use an 8x10). Sprinkle with bacon, spread with sour cream, and top with cheese. Sprinkle on a bit of paprika for garnish. Cover and refrigerate overnight. Reheat at 250°F for 25-30 minutes, or until cheese has melted thoroughly.

Strategies for Real Food Lunches and Snacks

I believe real food lunches should be quick, easy meals that you make, serve, and eat in a matter of minutes so you can get back to whatever your day is about–school, work, or play!

My husband comes home for lunch most days so, in our home, lunches are a sit-down family meal, much like dinner. This could mean spending that much more time in the kitchen every day fixing a full, nourishing meal at noon as well as breakfast and dinner.

But that's not the case (thank heavens) because of my lunch strategies:

Lunch Strategy #1: Leftovers

Leftovers are the save-the-day superhero of the real food kitchen, rescuing the cook from burnout on a regular basis. But leftovers don't just happen. They must be planned for and cultivated because they won't just show up out of thin air. I take care of lunch most days by simply making sure whatever I make for dinner the night before will serve my family twice. That way lunch is a simple matter of heating something up.

Lunch Strategy #2: Frozen Real Food

On the days when there just aren't leftovers, or we need a more portable lunch, I look to my pantry and freezer for prepared food that can become a quick lunch. I regularly keep pizza dough, bags of homemade tortillas, grated cheese, and leftover meat (like taco meat) in the freezer to have real food ingredients ready for quick lunchtime feasts. You can also freeze one loaf of bread (sliced) each time you make a batch and stock up on healthy lunch meats when they're on sale and freeze them so sandwiches are just a quick thaw away. A leftover quart of soup or chili is also a great thing to throw into the freezer for a future rainy or busy day.

Lunch Strategy #3: Embrace Simplicity

I look for lunch to give me and my family a solid protein, some good fats, and some unrefined carbs for lasting energy through the afternoon. If we can get that with some hot dogs (I love the nitrate-free beef ones) served on a paper plate (minus the roll, because I don't have time for that most days) and a bowl of yogurt with some fruit, that works for us. Lunch doesn't have to be fancy as long as it's nourishing. Other simple lunches for us include peanut butter and bananas rolled in tortillas, cheese and chips, or a simple quiche (check out Real {Fast} Food for two of our favorite quiche recipes).

But mostly, we just love us some leftovers.

Nourishing Snacks

By now we've seen the importance of good fats and plenty of protein for nourishing our bodies, so it's no surprise that our snacking habits may need adjusting. The biggest difference in how our family snacks now, compared to earlier in our journey, is that we go for nutrient-dense, body-nourishing foods, not just quick energy fixes. Grains and fruits fall further down the list of options, and we've gotten creative with how to make most of our snacks contain more protein, with a steady delivery of natural sugars to the blood stream.

Here's a list of nutrient-dense snacks to inspire you. If your family doesn't like some or all of these, keep exploring until you find what works for you. Just keep in mind that just plain fruit or refined grains will only provide a short energy spike, and our bodies need balanced snacks just like balanced meals.

- Cheese sticks
- Apples with nut butter
- Raw vegetables with homemade ranch dressing (see pg. 61)
- Yogurt with fresh fruit
- Dried fruit and nuts
- Leftover pancakes with nut butter
- Hard-boiled eggs
- Organic corn chips with hummus or cultured refried beans (see pg. 52)
- Leftover quesadillas

When we go out, I almost always grab something for our kids for snacks because I've learned that maintaining their blood sugar is crucial to a fun, successful outing. Since half of the above snacks require refrigeration, I keep a small cooler bag and an ice pack always ready, and quick snack fixings are at the top of my shopping list. Just like the strategy for easy, real food lunches, it helps to plan to make extra of something if it would work well as a snack later. Pancakes and tortillas make great vehicles for simple forms of protein like cheese or nut butter. For road trips or day trips, I take a little time to plan ahead, portioning yogurt into small, individual mason jars with toppings and a lid—just as convenient as the store bought ones, at a fraction of the cost.

When it comes to real food snacks, we need to be willing to think outside the box—literally. This may mean snack time is messier or takes a little more thought or preparation. But maintaining blood sugar and choosing nutrient-dense snacks will have long-term benefits for us and our families.

Macaroni and Cheese (pg. 92)

Real Food Dinner Favorites

Looking for real food dinners your family will actually eat? I'm all for nutrition, but I'm not real big on exotic ingredients or having my family refuse what I've cooked because it's too far outside their comfort zone. So my list of real food dinners focuses on familiar favorites built with nourishing, real food ingredients. They come together smoothly with flavor that has everyone–from husband to picky toddler–asking for seconds.

In this chapter you'll find two weeks' worth of real food dinner ideas—all favorites my family enjoys regularly. If you're not sure where to start with serving real food for dinner, try one or two of these recipes each week until you have your own collection of favorites. Remember to glance over your dinner plans at breakfast time and do one small thing to prepare for the evening meal!

> **Cultured Condiments**
> Suggestions for cultured condiments that go well with each meal will be found in these brown boxes. Remember to add cutlured condiments after you've served the food— you don't want to cook the enzymes!

Hearty Meatloaf

My family loves meatloaf. If your family have never been big fans, try this moist, flavorful loaf—and go ahead and serve it with some (high fructose corn syrup free) ketchup. We enjoy this loaf with creamy mashed potatoes and a steamed veggie, or baked sweet potatoes and a fresh salad. Leftovers are delicious sliced and fried in a bit of butter. This is an easy dish to double so you can pop one in the freezer for another day.

> **Cultured Condiment:** German Sauerkraut or Gingered Carrots.

- 1 c. whole milk
- 1 ½ c. rolled oats
- 2 lbs. ground beef
- 1 onion, peeled and finely chopped
- 1 carrot, peeled and grated fine
- 4 T. butter
- 1 t. black pepper
- 1 t. salt
- ½. t. thyme
- 1 egg
- 1 c. ketchup

Preheat oven to 350°F. Measure oats into a large bowl (or the mixing bowl on your mixer) and pour milk over to soften the oats. Meanwhile, peel and finely chop or grate your vegetables. Heat butter in a small frying pan and sauté onion and carrot until soft and golden. Add the sautéed vegetables, meat, and rest of ingredients to the mixing bowl. Knead on low or with your hands till mixed. Pat into a large loaf pan or a smaller casserole dish. Ice with ketchup. Bake at 350°F for one hour for a shallow casserole or 90 minutes for a loaf pan.

Creamy Mashed Potatoes

I love these potatoes because it simplifies the serving process—no passing all the condiments for baked potatoes and helping four children dress their potatoes while my own plate gets cold! It's also great for company because it can be made the day before.

- 8-10 medium potatoes
- 2 t. salt
- ½ c. butter
- 4 oz. cream cheese
- 1 c. sour cream
- salt and pepper to taste

Peel potatoes, cube and put in a large pot with enough water to cover and 2 t. salt. Bring to a boil and cook until soft. Drain off water, return potatoes to pot and use a hand mixer to beat them smooth, or transfer the potatoes to the mixing bowl of your stand mixer. When potatoes are completely smooth, beat in the rest of ingredients. Salt and pepper the potatoes to taste, then scoop them into a buttered casserole dish and pop into the oven for about ten minutes at 350°F to heat them through. You can also make them a day ahead, cover with aluminum foil, and reheat them covered for 20-30 minutes at 350°F.

Honey Baked Chicken

My older brother brought this recipe home with him after his apprenticeship at Joel Salatin's Polyface Farm fifteen years ago. It's been a favorite in our family ever since. We love this with a side of winter squash and rice or potatoes to sop up the drippings. Serves 6-8.

- one whole chicken, cut into parts, or 4-5 lbs. chicken legs and/or thighs
- ⅓ c. butter
- ¼ c. honey
- 2 T. yellow mustard
- 1 T. curry powder
- 1 t. salt

Place chicken parts in a 9x13 casserole dish. Melt butter and rest of ingredients in a small saucepan on low. Pour over chicken parts and bake at 350°F till golden brown, basting occasionally.

> **Cultured Condiment:** Gingered Carrots go great with the slightly sweet curry flavor of the chicken.

Simple Steamed Rice

I feed my family white rice because it is easier to digest than whole grain brown rice. The reason white rice is often avoided is because of its high glycemic index—I serve it with plenty of good fats to slow down its impact on our blood sugar. Frying the rice in butter first helps the rice to be fluffy and keeps the leftovers from caking into a clump of mush.

This recipe makes 8-9 cups cooked rice.

Melt 2 T. butter in a 3 quart or larger saucepan over medium heat. Add 3 c. rice and sauté, stirring frequently, until rice is fragrant and the grains have turned from slightly translucent to solid, creamy white (about 3 minutes). Add 6 c. chicken broth (or water) and 1 t. salt. Cover and set at medium low to bring to a simmer. If rice starts to boil, lower the temperature even more. Cook for 15-25 minutes until all liquid is absorbed and rice is soft and fluffy.

Beef Stroganoff

Most stroganoff recipes are either super involved with dozens of ingredients or else they cut corners by using canned soup. My recipe falls right in the middle with gourmet flavor and fast whole food ingredients. The credit to the tasty result all goes to good fats! Serves 6-8.

- 1 lb. ground beef
- 4-8 cloves garlic, minced
- ¼ c. butter
- 1 pkg. small fresh mushrooms, chopped
- ½ c. flour
- 1 c. chicken broth
- 2 c. whole milk
- 1 t. fresh ground pepper
- 1 t. sea salt
- 1 c. sour cream

Brown ground beef with the garlic in a 3-4 quart saucepan over medium heat. When brown, add the butter and the mushrooms. Cook, stirring occasionally, for 3 minutes or until mushrooms are wilted. Add the flour and mix it well into the meat and cook, stirring, for about a minute. Pour in the chicken broth and stir as the mixture thickens. Add in the milk and stir occasionally until mixture begins to simmer. Add the salt, pepper, and sour cream. When mixture is steaming hot again, remove from heat and serve over rice or pasta.

Cultured Condiment: Any meat/gravy combination deserves a bit of traditional German Sauerkraut on the side.

Seasonal Sautéed Vegetables

This is my method for gently cooking broccoli, green beans, Brussels sprouts, summer squash, or any other seasonal vegetable that comes my way.

Melt 2 T. butter or coconut oil in a medium frying pan. Meanwhile, rinse your vegetables and cut them into bite-sized lengths or slices. Add vegetables (still a bit wet from rinsing) to the pan and slap a lid on it. They will sauté and steam at the same time, getting the flavor of sautéing and the softness of steaming. Lift the lid to stir a few times, and when the vegetable's color intensifies, this means they're almost done. Add a few cloves of crushed garlic and a few tablespoons of soy sauce at this point if you like, and let cook for 3-4 minutes with the lid off if a lot of moisture has collected in the pan. When you can cut the vegetable with the edge of a fork, they're ready to be served.

Cheeseburger Soup

I don't know how I lived without this recipe in my repertoire. I love how it comes together with basic ingredients I almost always have on hand, yet has amazing flavor. Must be all the yummy, full fat dairy it calls for! Serves 6-8.

Cultured Condiment: German Sauerkraut or Kimchi.

- ¼ c. butter, divided
- 1 onion, chopped
- 3 carrots, peeled and grated coarsely
- 2-3 stalks celery, chopped fine
- ½ lb. ground beef
- 1 t. dried basil
- ¼ t. parsley
- 1 t. salt
- ½ t. pepper
- 3 c. chicken broth
- 4 c. potatoes, peeled and diced
- ¼ c. flour
- 1 ½ c. whole milk
- ½ c. sour cream
- 8 oz. cheddar cheese, grated

Melt 2 T. of the butter in a 3-4 quart saucepan. Chop the vegetables and throw them into the butter. Add the ground beef and break into small chunks with a wooden spoon while it cooks. Add the basil, parsley, salt, and pepper. When meat is browned and vegetables are tender, pour in the broth and the diced potatoes. Bring to a boil and then simmer for 15 minutes. Meanwhile, create a roux with the remaining 2 T. butter: melt butter in a small saucepan and stir in the ¼ c. flour and cook for about a minute, until mixture is bubbly. Pour into the soup and stir well. After roux has thickened the soup, add in the milk, sour cream, and cheddar cheese. Heat, stirring frequently, until cheese is melted, then it's ready to serve!

Frugal, Flavorful Chili

I love this recipe because it starts with simple ground beef, but by the time you're done adding spices, you'd swear it was sausage–so flavorful! Always served with a dollop of sour cream and a generous sprinkle of cheddar cheese around here. Easily serves 8-10.

If you want to make your own beans for this recipe, simply put a few cups of beans in a large bowl and cover them with water to soak overnight. In the morning, drain and rinse the beans, then cover with water again and cook on low in a Crockpot for 3-5 hours until soft. I make a large batch and freeze what I don't need immediately.

> **Cultured Condiment:** Cordito, Lacto-fermented Salsa or Cultured Refried Beans.

- 2 lbs. ground beef
- 4 T. butter, palm oil, lard or tallow
- ¼ c. red wine (optional)
- 2 c. beef or chicken stock
- 2 onions, chopped fine
- 2-4 small green chilies, hot or mild, seeded and chopped
- 2 24 oz. jars tomato sauce
- 3 cloves garlic, crushed
- 1 T. ground cumin
- 2 T. dried oregano
- 2 T. dried basil
- ¼-½ t. red chili flakes
- 1 T. chili powder
- 1 T. sucanat or sugar
- 4 c. cooked beans

In a 4 quart or larger saucepan, brown meat. Add onions, garlic, and butter (or lard or tallow) into browning meat. When onion is cooked, add the remaining ingredients. Simmer on low heat for an hour. Serve with cheddar cheese, sour cream, and your favorite Mexican style lacto-fermented condiment piled on top!

Moist Soaked Cornbread

This cornbread is so moist and yummy – no choking on crumbly coarseness wondering, "Whoever invented this stuff in the first place?" Of course, we cut the thick slices in half and butter generously and it's pretty much heaven in your mouth. Makes a 9x13 pan.

- 2 c. cornmeal
- 1 ½ c. whole wheat flour
- ½ c. honey
- ½ c. melted butter
- ⅓ c. yogurt, kefir, or buttermilk
- 1 ½ c. milk
- 3 eggs
- ½ t. salt
- 1 ½ T. baking powder

Stir the first six ingredients together (cornmeal through milk), cover the bowl, and let sit at least eight hours or overnight. (I'm usually making cornbread to serve with chili for dinner, so I start it in the morning while I'm cleaning up the kitchen from breakfast.) When you're ready to bake, preheat the oven to 375˚F. Grease a 9x13 inch baking pan. Add the eggs, salt, and baking powder to your batter. Mix it all together, pour into pan, and bake for 20-25 minutes until center is set and a knife inserted comes out clean.

Homemade Chicken Tenders

Get your chicken tenders fix at home with no added MSG or over-processed "meat product". In the summer I buy whole fryer chickens (it's the cheapest price per pound for chicken meat) and cut them up into parts—we use the dark meat for grilling, and I save the breasts for tenders. They make great picnic food! Serves 4-6.

- 2 large chicken breasts (about 1 lb. of meat)
- 1 egg
- ½ c. milk
- 1 c. flour (whole wheat or sprouted works fine here)
- 2 t. paprika
- 1 t. garlic powder
- 1 t. salt
- 1 t. pepper
- ½ t. dry mustard
- ¼ t. baking soda
- coconut oil, palm oil, or lard for frying (at least 1 c.)

Cube chicken into bite-sized pieces. Whisk the egg and milk together in a large bowl and add the chicken cubes. In another bowl, mix together the flour and spices. In a cast iron skillet or heavy-bottomed pot, heat the oil until a little bit of flour sprinkled in sizzles. Dip each piece of chicken into the flour mixture to coat, then place them in the pan. Cook on one side until brown, then flip the pieces with a fork. When the tenders are browned on all sides, check a fat one for doneness—cut it in half and if the meat is all white with no pink left, it's done! Drain the meat onto paper towels, and serve as desired. We love them tossed over romaine lettuce and doused with Caesar or honey mustard dressing. My babes usually skip the lettuce, but otherwise, this is a family favorite.

Honey Mustard Dressing or Dipping Sauce

Makes approximately ½ c.

- ¼ c. mayonnaise
- 2 T. yellow mustard
- 2 T. honey
- 2 T. olive oil (if making dressing)

> **Cultured Condiment:** Use your own Lacto-fermented Mayo in the dressing.

If making dipping sauce, combine mayonnaise, mustard, and honey and stir to combine.
For dressing, add the ingredients plus olive oil to a small glass jar and shake to combine. Leftovers will keep refrigerated for up to two weeks.

Fettuccine Alfredo

Cultured Condiment: Cordito.

This recipe takes a bit more focus in the kitchen because you can have three or four pots going at once, but it's nevertheless one of my quickest meals. We enjoy it with steamed broccoli and Italian sausage. Serves 4-6.

First, start a pot of water boiling for noodles. Then rinse your vegetables and put them in a steaming basket in a pot of shallow water to steam. Next, build your alfredo sauce.

Alfredo Sauce

- 4 T. butter
- 4 cloves garlic, crushed or chopped
- ¼ c. flour
- 3-4 c. milk
- 4 T. cream cheese.
- 1 ½ c. shredded parmesan cheese

Melt butter in a two quart sauce pan. Add garlic and cook until it begins to brown. Stir in flour with a whisk and cook until mixture is bubbly. Gradually pour in the milk, and cook, stirring constantly, until thick and bubbly (about 8 minutes). Add the cream cheese and cook for 2-3 more minutes. Finally, measure in the parmesan cheese and cook, stirring constantly, until cheese is melted.

While the sauce is thickening, you can start frying some sausage or heating up leftover chicken in another frying pan. Strain the pasta when done, and turn your vegetables off when they are fork tender.

Serve the alfredo sauce over fettuccine noodles with meat and vegetables on top, garnished with parsley and more parmesan.

Sloppy Joes

My favorite way to glorify ground beef. This is a favorite one I often double to put half in the freezer for a quick lunch on another day. Serves 4-6.

- 1 lb. ground beef
- 1 onion, chopped
- 1 T. chili powder
- 2 t. garlic powder
- 1 t. salt
- 1 t. ground pepper
- 1 T. yellow mustard
- ¼ c. sucanat or honey
- 2 T. vinegar
- 1 26 oz. jar tomato sauce

Cultured Condiment: You can top each sandwich with a bit of Gingered Carrots or German Sauerkraut.

Cook meat and onions together in a 3 quart pot until brown. Add rest of ingredients and stir to combine. Cook for 15 minutes, stirring occasionally. Serve over rolls with cheese and sauerkraut! (Okay, my husband thinks that last part is weird, but the kids love it.)

Soaked Yeast Rolls

If you're intimidated by the idea of making bread for the first time, why not start with yeast rolls? These are simple and fun, and a great way to try your hand at soaking dough. I start this first thing in the morning to have rolls done by dinner. It does require some additional flour to be added after the soaking period to adjust the dough's consistency—I recommend sprouted wheat flour or unbleached white flour. Makes 2-3 dozen rolls.

- 3 c. very warm water
- 4-5 c. whole wheat flour
- 4 T. whey, yogurt, or kefir
- ¼ c. soft butter or coconut oil
- 1 egg
- ¼ c. honey or sucanat
- 2 ½ t. salt
- 1 T. yeast, heaping
- 1-2 c. sprouted wheat flour or unbleached white flour

Combine water, 4 c. whole wheat flour, and whey or other cultured dairy in a bowl and mix thoroughly by hand or with a stand mixer. Add enough additional flour to bring the dough from batter-like consistency to a shaggy ball of dough. Cover and let soak for 6-8 hours.

Add butter, egg, honey, salt, and yeast and mix dough until incorporated. Add sprouted or white flour, ½ c. at a time, until dough begins to pull away from the sides of the bowl. Knead for about 5 minutes or until dough is smooth and elastic.

Cover bowl with plastic wrap and set dough in a warm spot (I use my porch in the summer, and the top of my fridge in the winter) to rise until double—about one hour. Punch the dough down by wetting your hand under cold water and squishing the dough back down into the bottom of the bowl. Let rise again for another hour (this is the secret to fluffy rolls!) and punch down again before shaping.

On a well-floured surface, pat or roll dough with a rolling pin until about one inch thick. Use a drinking glass as a cookie cutter to cut round, burger-style rolls. Place rolls side by side on a greased cookie sheet. Let rise for 30 minutes or until they've nearly doubled again. Bake at 350°F for 20 minutes, or until lightly browned.

Homestyle Chicken Noodle Soup

This classic comfort food comes together quickly and is a great use for leftover chicken. You can add any of your favorite vegetables, including green beans, corn, squash, or even spinach. Serves 6-8.

- ¼ c. butter
- 1 medium onion, chopped
- 2 large carrots, diced
- 2 celery ribs, diced
- additional vegetables of your choice
- ½ of 3 oz. can tomato paste
- 6 c. chicken broth
- ½ c. uncooked rice or 4 oz. pasta
- 2 t. salt
- ¾ t. pepper
- 2-3 c. cooked chicken, chopped

Melt butter in a 3 quart or larger sauce pan. Sauté onion, carrots, and celery until they are soft and golden. Stir in the tomato paste and any other vegetables you desire. Add chicken broth, rice/pasta, and salt and pepper and bring to a boil. Reduce heat and simmer, covered, for 30-35 minutes, until rice or pasta are cooked. Serve with a sprinkle of parmesan cheese.

Cultured Condiment: A few teaspoons of kimchi or German sauerkraut or even just the juice mixes invisibly into the soup and adds subtle flavor.

Homemade Rotisserie-Style Chicken

Take roast chicken up a notch with this flavorful rub. I serve this with potatoes, gravy, and steamed veggies. It's my favorite way to get leftover chicken meat for casseroles. (I usually do two birds to ensure leftovers.) Makes one whole roast chicken, or enough meat for 6-8 people.

- 1 whole roasting chicken (4-6 lbs.)
- 2 T. butter
- ½ onion, cut in quarters
- 4 cloves garlic, minced
- ½ a lemon (optional)
- 1 t. paprika
- 1 ½ t. salt
- ½ t. pepper
- ¼ t. chili powder
- 1 t. Italian seasoning
- ¼ t. thyme

> **Cultured Condiment:** Gingered Carrots or German Sauerkraut would complement chicken and fixings.

Preheat oven to 350°F. Remove giblets, rinse chicken, and pat dry. Place breast-side down in a metal skillet or roasting dish. Rub the outside of the chicken with the butter, and insert onion pieces, garlic cloves, and half a lemon (if desired) into the cavity of the chicken. Combine seasonings in a small bowl and then sprinkle them all over the bird, lifting a leg so you can chuck some in the cavity and get the back and sides of the bird too. Place in oven and set timer for 30 minutes. After the bird has cooked for 30 minutes, enough cooking juices will have dripped into the pan that you can start basting the bird every 15 minutes until it's done. (A 4 pound bird will take about an hour, a 6 pound bird about 1 ½ hours.) The bird is done when the leg bones jiggle loosely in their sockets, and a slice into the breast reveals all white meat and no pink. Lift the bird onto a serving dish so you can make gravy in the baking pan with the drippings.

Classic Chicken Gravy

Makes just shy of a quart of gravy.

- pan drippings from a roast chicken
- ¼ c. flour
- 3 c. chicken broth or water
- salt and pepper to taste

Heat drippings (liquid leftover from roasting a chicken) over medium heat in a skillet or metal roasting pan. Measure flour into a quart jar, add the broth or water, screw a lid on, and shake thoroughly to combine. Once the drippings are simmering, gradually whisk in flour and broth/water mixture, stirring constantly. Cook over medium heat until gravy begins to boil and thicken. Season to taste. (If made from the pan drippings of a rotisserie style chicken, it usually has plenty of flavor from the rub and there's no need to add more seasoning.)

Spaghetti Pie

I'm going to tell you how to make spaghetti pie completely from scratch, but please remember that this yummy dish is most easily made with leftovers! After your family has enjoyed platefuls of spaghetti and meat sauce, pull out some cheese and throw this baby together for a freezer meal or dinner later in the week. Serves 6-8.

- 12 oz. spaghetti (wheat or rice pasta)
- 1 lb. ground beef
- 1 small onion
- 2 cloves garlic
- 1 t. salt
- ½ t. black pepper
- 1 28 oz. can crushed tomatoes
- 1 16 oz. can tomato sauce
- 1 t. dried basil
- ½ t. dried oregano
- 4 oz. cream cheese
- ¾ c. shredded parmesan cheese, divided
- ¾ c. shredded mozzarella cheese, divided

Boil pasta according to package directions. Meanwhile, cook ground beef with onion and garlic until brown. Season with salt, pepper, and herbs, and add crushed tomatoes and tomato sauce. Simmer on low for 10 minutes. When noodles are done, drain them and put them right back in the pot. Stir the cream cheese into the hot noodles to melt it, and then add ½ c. each of the Parmesan and mozzarella cheeses, stirring to combine. Next add half the meat sauce over the noodles, mix, and pour noodles into a greased, 9x13 casserole dish. Pat the noodles down firmly with the back of a large spoon or rubber spatula. Pour remaining meat sauce over the top, then sprinkle with the rest of the cheese. Bake at 350°F for 20-25 minutes until bubbly and the cheese has started to brown.

Caesar Salad Dressing

My mom is famous up and down the east coast for her Caesar salad. She learned this recipe at a fancy restaurant in the Bahamas where the chef would make it right in front of her and my dad at their table. She ordered it repeatedly and took notes on a napkin until she got it just right. Makes just over one cup of dressing.

- 2-3 cloves garlic, minced
- 2 T. Dijon mustard
- 3 T. lemon juice
- 1 T. Worcestershire sauce
- 4 T. finely shredded parmesan cheese
- ¼ c. mayonnaise
- ½ c. olive oil
- ⅛ t. each salt and pepper

> **Cultured Condiment:** Use Lacto-fermented Mayonnaise in your dressing.

Add all ingredients into a wide mouth quart jar. Screw lid on tightly and shake. Wash a head of Romaine lettuce, shred, and place in large salad bowl. Pour dressing over and toss. Add more Parmesan and croutons, if desired.

Macaroni and Cheese

Mac and Cheese doesn't have a reputation as a nourishing meal, but I usually make mine with rice pasta and use whole milk and chicken broth in the cheese sauce. Throw in some leftover meat and veggies, and it's a complete and craveable meal. Taco meat and corn, diced ham and peas, chopped chicken and pesto—the possibilities are endless! Serves 6-8.

- 7-8 oz. macaroni pasta of your choice
- ¼ c. butter
- 4 T. flour
- 1 c. chicken broth
- 1 c. milk
- 8 oz. cream cheese
- ½ t. salt
- ½ t. pepper
- 2 t. brown mustard (like Dijon)
- 2 c. shredded cheddar cheese

Bring a large pot of salted water to boil. Cook pasta according to package directions. Meanwhile, in a 3 quart saucepan over medium heat, melt butter and stir in flour. Cook for about one minute, until smooth and bubbly, stirring occasionally.

Mix in milk, cream cheese, salt, pepper, and mustard. Continue cooking until sauce thickens. Add macaroni and cheddar cheese. Serve immediately, or add meat and vegetable of your choice to make it a complete one-dish meal. Transfer to a casserole dish and bake at 350°F for 15-20 minutes until golden and bubbly.

Spinach Salad with Berry Vinaigrette

Getting my kids, my husband, or even myself to eat salad, when there are yummy things like macaroni and cheese on the plate, can be a trick. This is our latest favorite recipe. I toss it over baby spinach with whatever salad additions I have on hand—grated carrot, raisins, nuts, feta cheese, chopped apple or fresh fruit. The kids actually ask for seconds! Makes just shy of one cup of dressing.

> **Cultured Condiment:** Add some gingered carrots to your salad.

- ¼ c. red wine vinegar (or juice from ½ a lemon)
- ¼ c. olive oil
- 1 t. brown mustard (like Dijon)
- 1 T. maple syrup or honey
- 1 clove garlic
- dash of salt and pepper
- ¼ c. fresh or frozen berries (strawberries, raspberries, and blackberries all work well!)

Combine all ingredients in a blender and blend until garlic is pulverized. Store in fridge for up to a week.

Sweet and Sour Meatballs

Cultured Condiment: Kimchi or Gingered Carrots go great with any Asian-inspired dish.

Enjoy your favorite sweet and sour flavor combo without all that MSG and high fructose corn syrup in the stuff you find at restaurants! This meatball recipe is also great for meatball sandwiches or spaghetti. Serves 6-8.

- 1 lb. ground beef
- ½ an onion, finely diced
- 1 egg
- ½ c. rolled oats
- 1 t. salt
- ½ t. ground pepper
- ½ t. crushed red pepper (optional)
- 2 c. chicken stock
- 2 T. soy sauce
- ½ c. sherry or white wine vinegar
- ⅓ c. honey or sucanat
- 1 T. arrowroot powder or organic cornstarch
- 2 T. butter or coconut oil
- 2 whole green bell peppers
- 1-½ c. fresh pineapple, or one 20 oz. can pineapple chunks

Preheat oven to 350°F. Mix ground beef, diced onion, egg, salt, pepper, oats, and crushed red pepper. Mix with hands until combined. Roll meat mixture into one inch diameter balls and place on a cookie sheet. Bake for 20-25 minutes until well browned. Meanwhile, mix together beef stock, soy sauce, sherry/vinegar, sweetener, and arrowroot powder/cornstarch.

Melt butter or coconut oil in a large frying pan on medium high heat. When pan is hot, throw in chopped green peppers and cook for one minute. Add the pineapple to pan and cook for one minute, stirring gently. Pour in stock/soy sauce mixture, then add meatballs. Stir gently to combine and allow to cook and bubble for a few minutes, or until sauce is thickened. Add more salt and crushed red peppers to taste. Serve over rice.

Enchiladas

This recipe is a little more involved, but if you're not ready to make enchiladas completely from scratch, choose one component at a time to add to your repertoire, okay? It's a perfect place to practice the "one step at a time" principle. I've made my own tortillas for years, but only recently have I found an easy enchilada sauce recipe that allows me to quit buying the MSG-laden cans from the store.

Green Enchilada Sauce

- ¼ c. fat of your choice (butter, coconut oil, lard)
- 1 large onion, chopped
- 1 pepper (hot, medium, or sweet, depending on your heat preference) or a 4 oz. can green chilies
- 2 cloves garlic, minced
- 2 T. flour or arrowroot powder
- 2 c. bone broth
- ½ c. chopped fresh cilantro (if you have it)
- ½. t. salt
- 1-3 t. chili powder
- 1 t. cumin

Sauté the onion, pepper, and garlic in the fat on medium heat until everything is well cooked and starting to brown. Stir in the flour or arrowroot powder, and then add the broth and cilantro. Cook until it thickens, then transfer to a blender to puree. Season with salt, chili powder and cumin to taste.

Enchilada Filling

You can use any sort of leftover meat and/or beans for enchiladas—just stir in some chili powder and cumin to flavor. If you're starting from scratch, here's what I do.

- 1 lb. ground beef
- 2 c. kidney or pinto beans (soaked and cooked, see pg.#)
- 1 t. salt
- 2 cloves garlic, minced
- 2 t. chili powder
- 1 t. cumin

Add all ingredients to a skillet and cook until meat is no longer pink.

> **Cultured Condiment:** Serve with Cultured Refried Beans, Lacto-fermented Salsa, Cordito, or all of the above.

Assembling the Enchiladas
- grated cheddar cheese
- seasoned meat
- enchilada sauce
- tortillas

Work on top of a tray or platter to catch the yummy mess you're about to make. Dip a tortilla into the enchilada sauce, coating both sides, then lay it on the tray. Spoon about 3 T. of meat filling and a sprinkle of cheese down the center of the tortilla. Roll up tortilla and lay, seam side down, in a greased casserole dish. Repeat until all the filling is used up. If you have any leftover enchilada sauce, pour it over the top of the rolled up tortillas. Then sprinkle a few handfuls of cheese down the middle of the pan for garnish. Bake at 350°F for 15-25 minutes until heated through and bubbly.

Soaked Whole Wheat Tortillas

I highly recommend purchasing an electric tortilla press if your family enjoys tortillas frequently—it will pay for itself in just months! You can roll these by hand, but it is much more time consuming. Makes 10-12 tortillas.
- 2 T. whey, yogurt, or kefir,
- 1 c. water
- ¼ c. coconut oil, butter, or lard, softened
- 1 egg yolk
- 1 t. salt
- 2-3 c. whole wheat flour

Begin by whisking the wet ingredients together, and then stir in the salt and flour. Add enough flour to form shaggy ball of dough. Do not knead. Cover bowl with plastic wrap and leave on counter for at least eight hours or overnight.

Spread your work surface with a tablespoon of olive oil. Scoop the dough onto the counter and roll it into a rough log so you can slice it evenly into 10-12 golf ball-sized chunks. Cover dough balls with a damp tea towel while you shape one tortilla at a time.

Using a rolling pin on a lightly floured surface, or a tortilla press, shape tortillas until they are 6-8 inches across. Immediately transfer hand-rolled tortillas from counter to a frying pan and fry over medium high heat until bubbles form, flip and cook a few more seconds until bubbles swell again, then transfer to wire rack to cool. Store stacks of tortillas in plastic storage bags in the fridge for up to a week, or freeze for later use.

Peanut Butter Cookies (pg. 100)

Nutrient-Dense Desserts

As we talked about in Chapter 8, sweets can have a place on the real food journey—in moderation and in combination with good fats and proteins. Here are some of my family's favorite nutrient-dense desserts that are great for the next time you have something to celebrate.

Fruit Crisp

I love making crisp because it's a quick way to enjoy whatever fruit is in season and is a lot less trouble than making pie crust. This basic recipe can be used with just about any fruit you have on hand—blueberries, blackberries, peaches, apples, and even rhubarb (which isn't a fruit, I know). Feel free to combine fruits and berries in the same crisp, as well!

Preheat oven to 350°F. Make the fruit layer:

- 3-4 c. fresh fruit, washed, and peeled and chopped if necessary
- 2 T. lemon juice
- 2 T. flour
- ¼ c. sucanat or dry sweetener of your choice

Mix together and spread in the bottom of a 9x13 baking dish.

For the topping:

- ½ c. flour
- 1 c. oats
- 1 c. sucanat or dry sweetener of your choice
- ½ c. finely chopped nuts (remember to soak and dry them! See Chapter 7)
- 1 t. cinnamon
- ¼ t. salt
- ½ c. cold butter

Combine dry ingredients in a bowl and cut butter into it with a pastry blender or two knives until mixture is crumbly. Pour over fruit layer. Bake for 35-40 minutes until topping is golden brown and fruit is bubbly.

Serve with a dollop of whipped cream if you have it, or even just a splash of whole milk.

Banana Split Smoothie

Turn a regular old smoothie into a milkshake-like treat with added maple syrup and chocolate. Full of pro-biotics and protein, dessert has never been better for you! Makes 3-4 cups.

- 2 c. kefir or yogurt
- 2 bananas (frozen, preferably)
- ½ c. natural unsweetened peanut butter
- 2 egg yolks*
- ⅓ c. cocoa powder
- 3-4 T. maple syrup (to taste)
- 6-8 bone broth (or plain) ice cubes

Combine all ingredients in blender and blend until smooth. Serve with straws.

Raw egg yolks from healthy, pastured hens are similar to raw milk—full of vitamins and enzymes when eaten raw. If you know your farmer and the eggs are clean, you need not worry about the diseases common in eggs produced in concentrated animal feeding operations (CAFOs).

Crockpot Tapioca Pudding

My kids adore tapioca pudding. I love serving it to them because it's rich in good fats and proteins. My friend and real food mentor, Claire, shared this simplest of methods with me. Serves 6-8.

- 2 quarts milk
- 1 c. small pearl tapioca
- ⅔ c. maple syrup or ¾ c. sucanat
- 4 eggs
- 2 t. vanilla

Stir first 3 ingredients in Crockpot and cook on high heat for 3 hours. Beat eggs and vanilla together in a small bowl and mix in a few spoonfuls of hot milk to temper the eggs. Stir back into Crockpot and cook 15-20 minutes longer. Put into a large bowl and chill completely before serving.

Peanut Butter Cookies

These cookies are grain-free and pack a solid protein punch! Makes 1 dozen.

- 1 c. smooth or crunchy peanut butter
- ½ c. sucanat (or natural sugar of your choice)
- 1 t. vanilla
- 1 egg

Cream all ingredients together and scoop rounded tablespoonfuls onto a cookie sheet. Flatten cookies with a fork in a criss-cross pattern. Bake at 350°F for 8-10 minutes until set. Let cool on wire racks.

Coconut Peanut Butter Fudge

- 1 c. coconut oil
- ½ c. peanut butter
- ¼-½ c. honey or maple syrup
- dash of salt
- 1 t. vanilla
- ⅓ c. cocoa powder

Melt coconut oil and mix in rest of ingredients. Pour into an 8x8 baking dish and cool in freezer. Cut into squares to enjoy—store in freezer to keep from softening.

Apple Crisp Cheesecake

Cheesecake is another great option for nutrient-dense dessert! This one takes it up a notch with an apple crisp-inspired topping. Remember not to be afraid of all the fat in cheesecake—full fat dairy is good for you! Make this with homemade cream cheese if you have it (see Chapter 4). Makes 10-12 servings.

Crust:
- 1 c. oats
- 2 T. sucanat (or other natural sugar)
- ¼ c. butter
- ¼ t. ground ginger

Pulse the oats in your blender or food processor a bit to make them finer. Reserve ¼ c. for topping. Melt the butter and stir it into the remaining ¾ c. oats with the ginger and sucanat (or sugar). Press mixture into the bottom of a 6 in. springform pan, or an 8x8 baking dish.

Filling:
- 2 8oz. packages cream cheese (or 2 c.)
- ¼ c. sucanat, maple syrup, or honey
- 1 egg
- ¼ c. sour cream
- ½ t. cinnamon
- ⅛ t. ground ginger
- 1 apple, peeled, cored, and thinly sliced

Beat cream cheese and sucanat until smooth. Add egg and beat just until combined. Stir in sour cream, cinnamon, and ginger. Pour over crust and arrange apple slices over top.

Topping:
- 3 T. flour
- ¼ c. reserved oats
- 3 T. sucanat (or other natural sugar)
- 2 t. cinnamon
- 2 T. cold butter

Combine flour, oats, sucanat, and cinnamon in a bowl. Cut in butter until crumbly. Sprinkle over apple slices.

Bake at 350°F for 40-45 minutes or until center is almost set. Cool at room temperature until no longer warm. Transfer to fridge and cool two hours or overnight before serving.

Enzyme-Rich Lemonade (pg. 56)

Tools You {Don't} Need for the Journey

We've covered a lot of ground so far on our journey, talking about a lot of tricks and techniques, and you may be thinking that baby steps we've taken so far are fine, but you're certain that pretty soon you're going to have to shell out some serious cash to get yourself the equipment you need to continue to make progress.

I've got good news.

Your kitchen does not depend on expensive appliances to produce real food. Yes, you'll probably see some fancy equipment in the photos of my kitchen on my blog, but I didn't always have a Vita-Mix, a grain mill, and a KitchenAid mixer, and I still don't have an Excalibur dehydrator. Before I acquired the appliances I do have (mostly through Christmas gifts, one year at a time), I made do with what I had, and you can, too!

Here's what to do if you don't have a fancy…

Blender

Many real foodies swear by their Vita-Mix, BlendTec, or Ninja blenders, and I admit that I adore my Vita-Mix and use it every single day. But here's the truth: the things I use it for most often can all be made in a regular blender.

Although capable of making nut butters and flour and chopping veggies, my blender gets used most often for smoothies and homemade mayonnaise, challenges even a cheap thrift store find could handle with aplomb. So, can't afford a $400 blender? Don't freak out. If your blender can manage a frozen banana and some flax seed, you're fine for lots of good real food.

KitchenAid/Bread Mixer

I'm quite fond of my KitchenAid (even named her Julia), but I consider her a luxury. See, I learned to cook when my family lived off the electric grid for nine years, and I did most things in the kitchen by hand because we didn't have any appliances. I beat egg yolks into stiff meringues for our annual strawberry torte with a vintage egg beater. I kneaded bread dough, grated cheese, chopped veggies, and stirred cookie dough all by hand. And it didn't kill me. Now, I use my KitchenAid every day, but I also know I can live without it.

The one thing I find I really appreciate a machine for is kneading bread dough–I just can't develop the gluten well kneading by hand without eventually adding so much flour that the bread becomes dry. So, back before I had my KitchenAid to knead my dough, I found a bread machine at the thrift store and used the kneading cycle on that to knead my weekly bread dough. This can be a very affordable option because bread machines were such a fad for a while and I see them all the time at thrift stores for as little as $10. Also, even if the heating element is shot, it still kneads dough well. So, can't afford a fancy mixer? Head to the thrift store for a bread machine!

Grain Mill

Now, this one is a little trickier, because, in my opinion there's nothing like fresh ground flour, and you are just not going to love your whole wheat baked goods as much with the rancid flour you'll get at the store. BUT grain mills are expensive, and you don't want to miss out on the joy and nutrition of freshly ground grains, so here are a couple ideas to get around the expense.

- Use your blender. Even a cheap blender can grind grain fairly well when combined with enough liquid ingredients as in batter for pancakes or waffles. (Our favorite blender pancake recipe is in my book, *Real Fast Food*)

- Learn to soak. Baked goods made from store-bought flour are denser and less flavorful. Lighten your loaves and boost the nutrition of those grains by using a recipe that incorporates soaking your grains.

- Borrow or co-op on a grain mill. A grain mill is one of those appliances you don't actually have to use every day, so you could realistically purchase one with a couple of friends and share it, grinding the flour your family needs for a week or a month and storing it in the freezer to keep it fresh.

My grain mill is an old hand-powered model my clever husband rigged to a motor. I love it, but it doesn't travel with us–too big and heavy. So, I make do with the above options when we're living on the bus. Eventually I'd love a Whisper Mill for when we're on the road.

Dehydrator

I don't have a fancy-shmancy dehydrator. Mine was rescued from an abandoned house, heats unevenly, and requires babying. But there are lots of ways to dry grain or fruit or nuts that don't require a machine. Simply spread whatever you're dehydrating on a clean window screen over a cookie sheet, and set in a toasty place like:

- in your oven on its lowest setting

- over a heat vent from your furnace in the winter

- under an old window pane in the sun in the summer

Food Processor

Two words, people: sharp knife. This is another lesson the homestead taught me. Anything a food processor can do, a good knife can accomplish. Yes, it can take a little longer, and maybe your onion won't be as finely and uniformly sliced, but a good knife is a fraction of the cost of an appliance, and it takes you far if you keep it sharp. I like my Pampered Chef Pro one with about a seven inch blade–I use it for everything from deboning chicken to dicing cabbage for sauerkraut. I don't actually get out the chopper attachments for my KitchenAid unless I'm preparing large quantities of food. That's because I hate doing extra dishes.

A Few More Appliances I Love for Real Food

So, those are my appliance hacks for the real food kitchen. It's not as expensive and intimidating as you thought, is it? In fact, if you save money by making do with one of the above ideas, you may have the cash to pick up one of these:

- Crockpot–wonderful because it allows you to prepare real food while you're sleeping (like bone broth).
- Tortilla Press–homemade tortillas are a mainstay around here, but I don't roll them by hand. Oh, no–I make them by the dozen in minutes with an electric tortilla press. (Visit the blog to see a video of me pressing tortillas and find out which brand I like.)
- Ice Cream Maker–there is nothing like homemade ice cream, and this toy means I rarely (like twice a year?) buy store-bought ice cream. I found one at the thrift store for a few bucks (score!)

To find out which brands I like and recommend, visit trinaholden.com/toolsforthejourney

Continuing the Journey

Seasonal Sautéed Vegetables (pg. 80)

The Seasonal Real Foodie

As we continue our real food journey, it's crucial that we learn to recognize the seasons along the way. No, I don't mean spring or summer—I'm sure you already understand the quality increase and savings you get when you buy food in season. I am talking about seasons in our lives.

We go through cycles in our lives: seasons of growth, seasons of rest, healing seasons, and survival seasons. We are more or less able to focus on what we've learned about better food choices depending on the season we are in. In order to continue to make progress and not become discouraged along the journey, we must know what season we are in, and embrace it. You can't fight seasons, so let's figure out what to do to accept and make the most of the season we're in.

Growing

This is the season you're probably in if you're reading this book. A growing season on the real food journey is often brought about by either a health crisis which has convinced you that you need to focus more on your diet, or a season in your personal life or family's needs that allows you a little extra time to focus on something new. You are excited and curious, reading books and blogs and discussing your discoveries with whomever will listen. You feel like trying new recipes, and you are energized by the idea of changing some things in your menu and routine. You learn new skills and quickly fit them into your routine. It's an exciting season! This season is often followed by…

Coasting

Life is good. You've changed a lot of things in your diet, and are maintaining your good habits. Life is a little too busy to learn any new techniques, but you feel good about the changes you've made so far, and your body and your family are thriving. This season may be followed by another season of growth, or interrupted by…

Survival Mode

You were doing well for awhile, there—but then life got crazy. You had a new baby, or lost a family member. Summer vacation caught you off guard, or school beginning threw you off balance. You changed jobs, relocated, the dishwasher broke, or some other major life event happened and suddenly you fell right off the real food wagon and found yourself in the checkout of the nearest fast food joint. You know you're not eating as healthy as you should, but there's no way in God's green earth you can cook dinner tonight, or be organized enough to make it to the co-op this month.

I'm going to climb on my soapbox right here and now and enunciate very clearly: *seasons are okay*. In fact, they are natural and good. Recognize them so you can go with the flow instead of fighting it.

If you are in a growth season, celebrate it! Do everything you can to grow and learn while you have the time and feel motivated. Sign up for that class, buy that book (and read it!), make a menu plan of new recipes, plan an outing to meet your local farmer. But realize that this kind of change and growth can't go on forever; it's like a growth spurt. You will level off, and that will also be okay. Don't beat yourself up if you feel like you're slowing down; it's a season, and seasons change.

Maybe you're reading this and you realize you're coasting right now. You just can't find the time or motivation to add anything new onto your plate. Please don't feel ashamed. If you're coasting, your job is to do so intentionally. Be aware of the season you're in, and plan to be faithful if an opportunity for growth presents itself. Keep doing what you're doing, and don't let the fact that you feel good or have lost weight lull you into thinking you can slack off on the good habits you've embraced. Stay faithful.

And if you're in survival mode? Once again I beg you not to spend energy on feeling guilty, but just ask that you be aware and as intentional as you can. The biggest thing to remember if you're in this season is that though we are called to steward our bodies well, what we put in our mouths is not the biggest influence on our health. No, the biggest factor in our health is the God who created our bodies. Trust this season to Him. Pray over your food and rest in the truth that the God who turned water into wine and fed five thousand with one boy's lunch can nourish your body with the food that's available to you. He operates outside of time and space and that plate of food you have no choice over is certainly under His jurisdiction.

Because our family travels a lot, and we seem to welcome a new baby about every two years, we've gone through our share of survival seasons in the area of food. Sometimes we're living on the bus with no local food connections, or I'm in bed with a newborn and I just can't feed my family as well as I know how to. In those seasons I try to hang on to a few basics, and then embrace the grace to let the rest go.

Tips for Survival Mode

1. A smoothie a day. Smoothies are quick and easy and give you that boost of raw foods and good bacteria that can help your tummy tackle whatever else comes down the pike.

2. Focus on protein. If you're stuck ordering from a take-out window or grabbing a packaged snack, make sure you choose something that will actually give you some sustained energy. Choose nuts, cheese and meat over grains or sweets.

3. Drink water. The temptation when we're on the go or feeling overwhelmed is to resort to fast forms of energy like coffee or soft drinks. Caffeine and sugar are only going to put more of a strain on your body, so stick to a drink that will actually help your body cleanse and run smoothly: just plain water.

Rediscovering Our Motivation

Then there are those days when we just lose heart. We are doing everything our schedule and budget will allow, but we still get sick. It seems like all of this effort is for nothing! My friend, Kristen, wrote about this very real frustration on her blog last year and I was so inspired by her words, I asked her if I could share them here.

About three-quarters of the way through the grocery store the other day, Micah started complaining of a stomachache. He was doubling over the steering wheel of the blue police car cart, so I asked Jonathan to take him to the bathroom, secretly thankful that I have a child old enough to escort his younger sibling to the bathroom so I don't have to drive those carts any farther than necessary.

Jonathan gladly trotted down the aisle with Micah at his heels. Two minutes later, Jonathan was back, face pale and eyes big. Micah was nowhere in sight. "Mom!" Jonathan gasped. "Micah just threw up all over the bathroom!"

Sure enough, Micah was standing in the middle of the men's bathroom covered in all the loveliness of the stomach flu. I cleaned him up as best I could, summoned a poor pock-faced boy with a bucket mop who looked at me like I had just ruined his life, snagged four dozen organic eggs, then rushed home before Micah could use the double grocery bags we gave him to hold under his mouth in case of a repeat incident.

The stomach flu is like Ground Zero for Mommyhood. Is there anything worse? Of course there are worse things, but I don't want to talk about it right now because my kids have the stomach flu and I just know all those germs are crawling all over me and I hate throwing up like nothing else in all the world.

Allow me a moment to feel sorry for myself.

I feed my kids well, make sure they get plenty of sleep, smear all kinds of oils on their feet and noses and chests, dole out vitamins like a pharmacist, mix up kefir and kombucha and sprouted things for their benefit…and still. We got the flu this week.

This, on top of our nearly six-week bout with strep, makes me feel defeated. How can a healthy family be so unhealthy?!

As I switch loads of sheets in the wash I remind myself that I do not maintain a healthy lifestyle so that we don't ever get sick. (It's a good thing, too, since there's a pretty good chance we have the plague).

I maintain a healthy lifestyle because I believe it is the best way to care for the little bodies God has given me. It is the best way I can ensure they are physically able to live up to the potential God has for them.

It is my gift to their adulthood.

I believe I can nourish them now so they can better live life better later, without the complications that result from an unhealthy lifestyle.

By God's grace, my children will have a healthy relationship with food, an appetite and appreciation for real ingredients and whole foods, solid immune systems, an understanding of the cycle of sickness, and a knowledge of natural remedies. They will have strong bodies and clear minds. They will know how to make healthy choices on their own, and they will understand why it is so important to do so.

They will come down with stuff. They are kids, after all, and kids smear all the germs on all the stuff and then put all the stuff in their mouths. It's amazing any of them survive.

Sickness is just part of the deal, and that's okay because I am confident that God has made their bodies well, and I believe that in most instances, their bodies can heal themselves if given the rest and resources they need.

I don't do this so we won't ever get sick.

I do this because I believe it's the very best way to live.

Kristen Glover—fiveintow.com

Kristen's story reminds us of an important principle on the real food journey—it's a process, and a long one at that. What you're doing today is not always going to have results tomorrow. Eating healthy this month will not guarantee you'll avoid the sniffles next month. We fool ourselves when we think we have that much control over things. Eating healthier is not really about how we feel today or next month. It's about building long-term health.

If you've found yourself discouraged at your lack of "progress", thinking that surely by now all the effort you've put into real food should be netting you some measurable results, please step back a moment and get a change of perspective. Just as changing your eating habits takes time, the fruit of those changes also takes time. Don't let short-term setbacks distract you from the long-term goal. Continue to learn what you can, grow when you can, and build habits that build strong bodies in the long run.

The Ultimate Breakfast Smoothie (pg. 66)

How to Gain Companions on the Real Food Journey

My husband hasn't always been on the real food bandwagon with me. At the beginning of my journey, when I was researching, educating myself, and brewing kombucha, he was drinking Pepsi. But now he's the one who drives a three hour round trip to purchase our raw milk supply for the month!

What changed? And how did we keep food from coming between us when we weren't quite on the same page?

It was a process, for sure. It took me being willing to make two dishes for dinner sometimes. Of having things in the house that I wouldn't eat, but blessed him. It took patience and determination. But eventually my analytical, logical husband came around because, he said, "Real food makes sense."

Three Tips for Getting Your Family on the Real Food Bandwagon

Tip One: Be a good example

Often the biggest influence on people's health habits is not a book or blog they read, but a relationship. (For me it was my crunchy friend, Claire.) Be that person for your loved one! Cook yummy wholesome meals for them, drink your weird concoctions in front of them, and let them observe the difference healthy choices are making in how you look and feel. Notice this tip does not require talking—you're just living it out in front of them.

Tip Two: Educate

You probably love to research and read whole books on the subject of healthy diets, which means you can give your friend the gift of gleaning the choice tidbits so they can learn along with you without being overwhelmed. (I use car rides with my husband to read the latest blog post that's inspiring me.) This tip does involve talking, but you can avoid nagging by sharing the information once from a valid source and then letting them assimilate it on their own time table.

Tip Three: Be patient

We call this the real food journey for a reason: it's a process. Some people are going to take leaps and bounds, others will be more like tortoises about the whole thing. But remember who won that race? My husband is the type to think things over for years sometimes before he takes action. But when he does, it's a well thought-out, permanent change. It's worth the wait.

Do Real Men Eat Real Food?

Often a guy's reluctance to make healthy changes comes from a fear that they'll have to start eating rabbit food at every meal and never see a juicy steak again. But you and I know different.

For the last 50 years, our culture's idea of healthy food has been piles of vegetables, with meat and dairy only if it's been stripped of fat. But lately we've been (re)learning that to truly nourish our bodies we need plenty of protein and good fats—after all, that's what our bodies are made of! The "new" healthy diet (inspired by our ancestors, rather than the profits of the commercial food industry) is full of flavorful meats, rich sauces made from bone broths and good fats, and satisfying dairy products that rejoice the palette while deeply nourishing our bodies.

Vegetables have their place, but it's no longer center stage.

So, the secret to men embracing real food? Sock it to them! Next time the man in your life says he's just not interested in eating healthier, make him a steak or a big fat meatloaf. Serve it with potatoes that have been whipped with butter and cream and seasoned with real salt. Add some steamed vegetables swimming in more butter (to help you assimilate all the fat-soluble vitamins!). Finish the meal with homemade ice cream made with whole milk from grass fed cows.

Then inform him he's just eaten "health food".

Another great way to get your spouse into real food is to show them how much money it saves a family! We'll talk more about that in the next chapter.

Real Food for Real Kids

The next question you may have is, "Do your kids really eat all this real food you make?" Usually. Mostly because I focus on finding meals that are both nourishing and yummy. It's a waste of time and money for me to make something they won't eat, but we do have a wide variety of meals they eat well. "Well" being a relative term depending on the mood we're in, if the littles have had naps, and if I let them snack before dinner. Here are my top tips…

Serve small portions

The great thing about having nutrient-dense food at every meal is that even if I only get my kids to eat a few bites, I know they've been nourished. A little bit goes a long way. We have a rule if they don't feel like eating, they have to take as many bites as they are old. For Seth, that's just three bites, which he counts himself and isn't overwhelmed by. Jesse has to eat seven bites, which usually comes close to emptying his plate! (Sneaky mama scores again!) We have raw milk with almost every meal, so that kind of fills in the gaps with good protein, fats, and the grass fed goodness that comes through the milk when the cows are on pasture. When we don't have raw milk, kefir smoothies made with milk from the local pastured herd are a near-daily habit.

Make it fun

My kids are not big on soup. We have to get creative when their soup-craving mama serves dinner in bowls. Last winter when I made my favorite chicken vegetable soup I called it Amazon Stew because we'd just been studying about the Amazon Jungle in school. Suddenly it became a contest to see who could eat a crocodile (green beans!) or a goldfish (corn!) or a great big boa constrictor (noodles!). Now they play the game whenever I serve that soup, and we have much fewer complaints.

Reward them

We use bribery regularly. I know that sound awful, but it's really not. They have to eat their breakfast eggs before they get their toast or fruit. They have to eat their soup before they get cornbread. They have to eat at least half the food on their plate before they get a drink with their meal, otherwise they fill up their bellies with liquid and have no room for food. And no dessert until plates are clean. Just good old-fashioned training.

Hide the weird stuff

The other thing they don't eat well is sauerkraut, so I just sneak the milder versions, like gingered carrots or cordito, in with something before I serve it to them and they don't notice. They get most of their enzymes from kefir smoothies and bowls of yogurt. I hide lots of goodies like fermented bean paste, Mexican sauerkraut, and sprouts in taco salad.

Let them help

They are way more willing to eat something, or at least try it, if they helped make it. My seven-year-old helps me sprout, dehydrate, and grind grain, sprout seeds, feed our sourdough starter, chop veggies for sauerkraut, and especially lick the spoon when we make peanut butter fudge. All my children have a more open mind about new foods if they helped find it at the farmers market and were somehow involved in the making of it.

Making Progress Together

When you're trying to take a whole family on the real food journey, there will invariably be things you don't all agree on—taste and texture preferences are very real! I've come to realize that the more people you're trying to feed, the more variety you may need to have in your fridge or your menu plan. Although I don't treat meal times like a restaurant and cook something different for everyone, I do try to take my kids' and my husband's preferences into consideration as I menu plan, and if I know a main dish is not well-tolerated by one person, I try to offer a side to fill out the meal for them.

Do we ever "cheat" and eat food that isn't ideal? Oh, my goodness, yes. I live in the real world, people. I am not a fake person hiding behind perfect-looking blog posts. (Wait till you hear about the cake I make in Chapter 19!) Reality has its effect on our diet. We travel a lot. When we do, we eat in–gasp!–restaurants! (I love Chick-fil-A!)

Our goal is to eat as healthy as we can when we're at home, so we don't have to stress about food when we're out and about. Some call this the 80/20 rule—eating as well as you can 80% of the time, so you don't have to stress about the 20% you have no control over.

This doesn't mean we binge when we hit the road–my kids drink water (not soda) in restaurants. We almost never order dessert. We focus on protein and not carbs in our meal choices. We give ourselves grace. I can't control everything we eat, and because we don't have any allergies, I don't have to. I do my best, and let it rest.

Instead of every single thing being a major issue, I have a short list of stuff I don't budge on, and embrace grace for the rest. One thing we do not do is food coloring. My kids have this so rarely that when they do they go insane. So even when it's a dear relative trying to serve a tasty dessert to my kids at a holiday get-together, I gently put my foot down if it's got food coloring, and explain that it makes my kids crazy. No one really wants crazy kids, so I don't get flack. I've talked with my kids about the effect certain foods have on their system, and they are learning to choose what makes them feel good and avoid the foods that will literally keep them awake until midnight.

Openly discussing the why behind your food choices is important, but so is remembering that each family member is on their own individual journey to stewarding their bodies. If you have older children, I'd encourage you to feed them as well as you can when they are at your table, and make a book like *Nourishing Traditions* by Sally Fallon part of their assigned reading list or family discussions. Even if they are already making their own food choices, you can still give them the gift of understanding how their bodies work and what foods will nourish them. They may go through a season of eating junk, but if they have real food knowledge, they will know what to turn back to when they finally realize they need to eat healthier.

Herbal Seasoned Salt (pg. 60)

How Real Food Actually Saves You Money

Hopefully by this time you're beginning to get an idea for how simple it could be for you to make some changes in the way you eat. You've seen how it's possible to fit real food prep into a busy schedule, you've got ideas for how to get your family on the same page, and you've got some great recipes for breakfast, lunch and dinner. But in the back of your mind is the nagging question,

"Can I really afford the cost of switching over to real food?"

In this chapter I want to explain how most of the steps I've outlined in this book can actually *save* you money. Here are four areas a real food approach can actually bless your budget:

Supplements

First, real food saves you the cost of dietary supplements. When you're eating whole foods, properly prepared, they provide so much more nutrition than all those pills and vitamins we've been taught are necessary. When you are slathering your veggies with butter, you're encouraging better assimilation of fat-soluble vitamins A, D, E, and K. When you sprout a seed or grain, the nutrient count skyrockets. When you make your own cultured dairy, condiments, and vegetables you're getting a wide range of beneficial enzymes and probiotics that aid digestion, allowing proper absorption of everything else you're eating. And the vitamins in food are recognizable and easily utilized by your body, whereas many supplements are made with manufactured nutrients that you can't even absorb.

A friend called me the other day in distress because she simply could not afford the expensive probiotics she'd been encouraged to take. I calmed her by asking her to list all the cultured and fermented things I knew she was eating regularly (water kefir, kombucha, and yogurt) and then, knowing she loves sauerkraut, promised I'd make her a jar each of cordito and German sauerkraut when I tackled the cabbage in my fridge. It's the same thing as the pills, but in food form, made from affordable ingredients as simple as cabbage!

The switch to whole foods can actually save you hundreds of dollars in dietary supplements.

Processing

The second big savings is in the processing.

- A quart of good quality milk costs anywhere from $0.75 to $2.50.
- Good quality yogurt made from whole milk costs upwards of $4.75 per quart.

Do you see where I'm going with this? If I am willing to heat that quart of milk and stir in one ingredient, I can save myself up to $4 with every quart of yogurt we consume! By simply being willing to prepare a portion of your food from scratch, you can save significantly on the cost of processing. What other foods can you easily prepare and save money on? Bone broth is another big one–you use bones you would otherwise throw away, plus water, to make a real food superstar (while you sleep!), the equivalent of which would cost you $2.50 *per 8oz.* if you had to purchase it!

Switching to eating more real food can actually mean significant savings if you make the full switch from buying prepared foods to learning to cook for yourself. This principle applies across the board, from bread and cookies to vegetables and condiments. Learn to prepare, process, and preserve your own food to trim your grocery budget even as you perhaps spend more for quality ingredients.

Packaging

Back to the yogurt example. Every time you buy a carton of yogurt, you're paying for a plastic container you throw away (or recycle if you're awesome like that). Every time you make homemade yogurt, you can use the same glass jar over and over and over again.

Switching to whole foods–stuff that can be purchased around the perimeter of your grocery store or from your local farmer–cuts down on the expense of all that fancy packaging you find in the center aisles. Buying in bulk from a co-op also means fewer containers, less plastic, less waste, and less cost. We rarely think about this expense, but it's a hidden cost in nearly everything we buy!

Healthcare

Finally, I've saved the best for last. This one isn't as easy to quantify, but it is probably the biggest place you'll end up saving money as you embrace eating healthier. When you nourish your body well, your body will function the way God designed–your immune system will fight off disease, cells will regenerate, and you will have the energy to live a full, thriving life. You may feel so good, you'll forget your doctor's name. (Or, like me, not even have a doctor!)

I know that's a hefty promise, and there are a lot of variables that will mean different outcomes for every family, but the general principle applies: eat healthier, and you'll be healthier. Less trips to the doctor or dentist, less co-pays, cheaper insurance, less anxiety, and a lot more time to enjoy life, your family and delicious, nourishing food.

God has blessed our family's health, and I believe real food has been a tool He's used. My kids have never been to the doctor. We rarely get sick and when we do, our immune systems kick it within a few days. We have no allergies, no ongoing conditions, and no learning disabilities or behavioral conditions. They are healthy and strong and Mom and Dad have the energy to keep up with them (most days!). Getting to this point takes time and commitment (we made the switch to a Weston A. Price inspired diet when my eldest was about a year old, so going on seven years) and you may have to go through a season of a stricter, healing diet (like GAPS). However, eventually I do believe you will find that a nourishing diet will have a significant positive impact on your health.

I guess the real question is not "Can you afford to switch to real food?", but rather, "Can you afford *not* to?" Most of the changes I walked you through in this book will not significantly impact your budget, so why not give it a try?

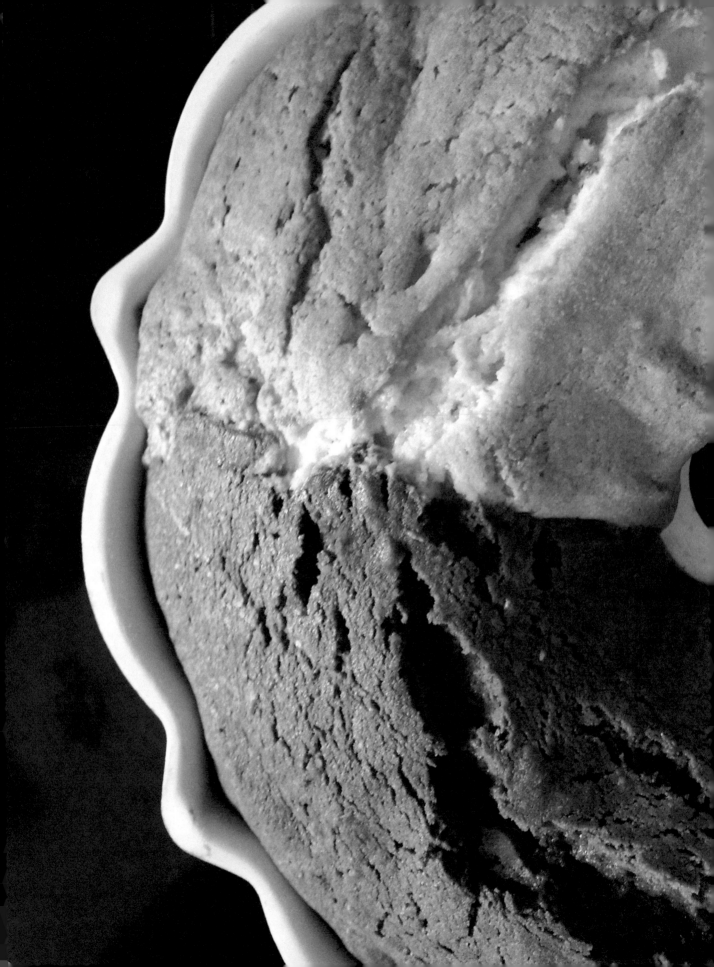

Enjoying the Journey

I began my real food journey just over nine years ago. It started with a nerve-wracking trip with my mom to her naturopath to find out what in the world was wrong with me. I had the recovering-hypochondriac's hope that my symptoms were all in my imagination, but a blood test and the naturopath's analysis said otherwise. My hair loss, irregular cycles and those strange moles on my back (more appearing every day!) all pointed to the fact that my body was under severe stress, and I was falling apart, inside and out. She said my liver looked like that of an alcoholic (though I didn't drink!) and she was very concerned.

It would be two more years before we got to the root cause of the stress (an anxiety disorder), but some key diet changes could be made right away to reduce the stress my whole body was under. White flour and sugar were out immediately. Later I'd cut out grains for a whole six months. I'd have to change my entire approach to foods, for though I was raised on home-cooked meals, all those whole grains and a misunderstanding of proper preparation were taking their toll on my gut. I wasn't getting enough protein, and Candida was also trying to overwhelm my system.

Nevertheless, I left her office with a feeling of peace because of the Candy Bar Principle.

I heard it over and over from this dear lady, and from other friends who went to see her. Even as she diagnosed, instructed, and mentored people toward healing through nutrition, she was constantly speaking this grace-giving truth to us:

"Stressing about what you eat is as bad as eating a candy bar."

Sink your teeth into that one, caramel and all, will you? *Because it's truth.*

Studies have shown and personal experience confirms the ill effect mental stress has on our physical well-being. As we begin to learn about healthier choices and dietary changes that we may have to make, the stress can begin to mount. But we should make every effort to let go of the stress as it comes, because the strain stress has on our bodies can be as unhealthy as something we're allergic to or a serving of junk food.

But how do we let go of that stress, with the pressure to reform, the challenge of sourcing new foods, the attempt to learn new recipes and the information overload of the real food movement? How do we keep from freaking out when we finally learn the foods to pursue or avoid, but they're too lofty a goal for our time or budget?

The Real Secret to a Stress-Free Real Food Journey

The secret to remember is that the biggest factor in our health is not our own efforts–it's the God who created our bodies. God may very well be leading you to understanding your body better, calling you to become a better steward of your health and to make wiser choices for what you feed your family. But never at any point does He lay the entire responsibility for our health on our efforts. Through whatever challenge we face, God maintains His role as Creator and Sustainer of our bodies, reminding us that while we can't change a hair on our head, He has our hairs numbered.

So, as we continue your real food journey, remember the Candy Bar Principle. Remember that if you start to stress out about a challenge you face along the way, not only are you stressing your body further, but you're forgetting the truth that we have a Maker who is also a Healer. He's walking this journey with you. So, relax–and...

Don't eat that candy bar.

The Art of Compromise

Once upon a time, not too long ago or far away, I made a pound cake.

With white flour and sugar.

Does this shock you? Have I completely lost my credibility as a real food blogger?

I hope not, because I have a really important point to make with this story.

We were living in our converted bus at that month. I was making a pound cake for my son's birthday because it only required very basic ingredients, and would be yummy enough without frosting (with a kitchen the size of a closet, it's all about simplicity on the bus).

Problem: half of our family loves chocolate. The other half don't (*I know, I don't get it, either*). Personally, I was craving chocolate, but didn't want to make a dessert that only half the party would enjoy. So, *I compromised.*

I mixed up a lovely vanilla pound cake, and poured half of the rather thick batter into the pan. Then I stirred in a heaping measure of cocoa powder into the remaining batter, and poured that into the other half of the pan. It was a beautiful marriage of delectable batters, and it baked up beautifully. I wish you could have smelled it, let alone tasted it. Everyone was delighted (including the birthday boy).

What does this cake have to do with your real food journey?

There will be days when you will struggle to please both parties–the voice in your head that is full of your accumulated real food knowledge, and the voice of reality that says you only have so much time or money or energy–they will be at odds with each other. You will have to make a choice that is a nod to both your ideals and your reality. You will have to compromise.

And you know what? It will be okay. You will live. You will not die from one white flour/white sugar pound cake. Life will be full and rich and sweet. Stress need not flavor every meal you make.

So, as we close this book, my final piece of advice to you is this: Be intentional in your food choices for your family, realizing that compromise will be a regular part of the process. The fact that you are making the effort to become more conscious of healthy eating habits is key, even if it doesn't show up in every meal from this moment on. Real food is a process–let your goal be to embrace the journey.

Let's journey together!

Now that we know that eating well isn't a target we have to hit the first time, but a journey we go on together, let's spread the good news! You can remind yourself of this refreshing perspective and encourage your friends if you share your journey with the hashtag #myrealfoodjourney. Let's quit condemning ourselves and celebrate the progress we've made so far, because every step counts and it's more fun together.

If you love this book, adore one of the recipes, or otherwise find this book to be an encouragement for your real food journey, share it with friends! Use the hashtag #yourrealfoodjourneybook on photos you share on social media. If you would like to host a giveaway on your blog, or inquire about wholesale pricing to become an encouraging resource for your own friends send me a note at http://trinaholden.com/contact/

Index of Recipes

Dinners

Acknowledgements

This book happened because of my husband. Because I didn't even know how to turn on the laptop he bought me to write this book on. He is my tech support, voice of reason, intentional father to the children of a distracted mother, and every moment that I write is a gift from a man who'd really like me all to himself. Thank him when you see him, ya'll.

Thanks to Ladder Bloggers—my mastermind group who honestly and lovingly encourage and critique my every brainstorm and overlook typos to value the heart behind my writing. They bear the brunt of all my insecurities when launching a new project, and they were the first ones to love this book with encouraging photos and tweets.

To the women who worked tirelessly on this book while in the editing stage—Jessica, Claire, and Gretchen. You gave more to this project than I had the audacity to ask for, showing me again what a faithful Provider our Father is.

To Caroline and Jewliet, sweet sisters who got up before the sun to snap a photo on a back road in Texas, and provided the beautiful 'clothes' for my book to wear into the world.

To my blog readers. I'm afraid I'm a better author than blogger—I post sporadically, neglecting you and yet when I peek out of my test kitchen or writing fog, you're there cheering me on, taking my recipes and making memories with your families, and letting me live my dream of encouraging others toward a thriving life.

Thanks to all my in real life friends who put up with my intense personality and obsession with cooking from scratch. To Laura, whose enthusiasm for my real food coaching confirmed my calling to write another cookbook. To Jeni, who groans with pleasure at my lunch table and generously shares wisdom to help me steward my calling. To Katie, who prays and asks hard questions. To Rebekah, who calls me 'friend' and makes me laugh. Every time.

And thanks to my Father God, who gave us the freedom and privilege of stewarding our bodies, and for making food more than fuel, but an experience that delights the senses and nourishes body and soul.

About Trina

Trina lives in NE Alabama with her husband and four children. She is a culinary gypsy, collecting treasures from each stop on the journey. She gained her love of cooking in her teens, preparing food for six siblings over an open fire on a working homestead. She caught the vision for more nourishing techniques during health struggles in the early years of her marriage. And she continues to find joy in the challenge of making meals that are both good and good for you while homeschooling, blogging, and traveling in their converted bus. Her favorite foods are avocados, heavily buttered rolls, and chocolate. Trina loves hospitality and cooking for crowds, and is always ready to set one more place at the table! At trinaholden.com she writes about food, freedom and other ingredients for a thriving life.

Real {Fast} Food

Plan better
Cook faster
Eat healthier

Trina Holden

Real {Fast} Food is a treasure trove of time saving techniques and simply wonderful recipes that are custom fit for you and your schedule. You'll learn everything from painless freezer stocking and bulk food prep to quick, healthy meals for day trips. Trina will teach you how to think about whole food prep in a whole new way, allowing you to make more real food in less time than you ever imagined, and even giving you the feeling of a "day off" once in a while -- all without sacrificing quality.

Over 60 pages of inspiration and practical how-to for streamlining real food prep. Find recipes for Trina's whole wheat, soaked pizza dough, favorite make-ahead casseroles and crockpot meals, and 50 more delicious, whole-food recipes. Plus menu planning and bulk shopping tips and bonus printouts to get organized.

All recipes are time tested and approved by family and friends. They're based on broths, soaked grains, good fats, and natural seasonings and sweeteners.

Available in paperback, PDF, Kindle or Nook, Real {Fast} Food is your ticket to fitting real food into your busy schedule!

http://trinaholden.com/realfastfood/

Made in the USA
Columbia, SC
05 November 2024

45667328R00082